Raise Children After Divorce

A Step-by-Step Guide to Create Stability and Strengthen Finances for a Healthy Co-Parent Relationship

Author: Daniel McMahon

Copyright ©2025 All rights reserved.

No part of this publication may be copied or reproduced in any format, by any means, electronic or otherwise, without prior consent from the copyright owner of this book.

Self-Published: Daniel McMahon
ISBN: 978-1-7640288-0-6

Author: Daniel McMahon

DEDICATION

This book is for all parents navigating the complexities of co-parenting after divorce.

Your strength and resilience are remarkable to the mothers, fathers, grandparents, and caregivers who strive to create a stable, loving environment for their children in the face of challenges.

To my children, who have taught me more about love, patience, and perseverance than I could have ever imagined. This journey would not have been possible without you.

And to every family that has faced the trials of separation but continues to choose love, understanding, and growth, you are not alone. May this book be a beacon of hope, a guide to smoother waters, and a reminder that the family remains at the heart of change.

With all my love and admiration.

Daniel McMahon

TABLE OF CONTENTS

DEDICATION 5

INTRODUCTION 9

CHAPTER 1 11

Understanding the Emotional Landscape

CHAPTER 2 23

Effective Co-Parenting Communication

CHAPTER 3 33

Legal Navigation Simplified

CHAPTER 4 43

Financial Stability After Divorce

CHAPTER 5 53

Age-Specific Parenting Strategies

CHAPTER 6 63

Building Emotional Resilience in Children

CHAPTER 7 73

Blended Family Dynamics

CHAPTER 8 83

Extended Family Involvement

CHAPTER 9 93

Self-Care for Parents

CHAPTER 10 103

Practical Tools and Strategies

CHAPTER 11 113

Future-Focused Parenting

CHAPTER 12 123

Encouragement and Reflection

CONCLUSION 133

ABOUT THE AUTHOR 137

SOURCE MATERIAL 138

INTRODUCTION

"I never thought I'd be here, navigating the uncharted waters of co-parenting after divorce. But here I am, and if you're reading this, chances are you're in the same boat. We're not alone—according to recent statistics, nearly half of all marriages in the United States end in divorce, leaving countless parents facing the daunting task of raising their children across two households.

I felt overwhelmed, scared, and utterly unprepared when I embarked on this journey. How could I ensure my children's well-being while managing the emotional fallout of my own failed marriage? I searched high and low for a guidebook, a roadmap to help me navigate this new terrain, but I couldn't find one that spoke to me personally.

I wrote this book—to provide the resource I wish I had when I first started co-parenting after divorce. It's not just a collection of facts and figures; it's a heartfelt, honest look at the challenges we face as divorced parents and a toolkit of practical strategies to help us overcome them.

Whether you're a mom, dad, or grandparent, this book is for you. It's for anyone who wants to create a stable, nurturing environment for their children, even during the chaos and heartbreak of divorce. We'll dive into the emotional, practical, and developmental aspects of parenting in a two-household family, exploring everything from managing conflict with your ex to supporting your children's mental health.

Each chapter will be a stepping stone on your path to successful co-parenting. We'll start by understanding our emotional responses to divorce and how they impact our parenting. Then, we'll move on to practical strategies for communication, decision-making, and creating a cohesive parenting plan. Finally, we'll look to the future, exploring how to adapt our co-parenting approach as our children grow and our lives change.

Throughout the book, you'll find real-life examples from my co-parenting journey and insights from other divorced parents who have been where you are.

But this book isn't just about information—it's about transformation. It's an invitation to shift your perspective, to see co-parenting not as a burden but as an opportunity for growth and positive change. By actively engaging with the content and applying the strategies provided, you'll take a bold step towards creating the harmonious, supportive family environment your children deserve.

I won't sugarcoat it—co-parenting after divorce is hard work. There will be moments of frustration, sadness, and doubt, but there will also be moments of joy, connection, and triumph. This book is your companion, offering guidance, support, and a reminder that you're not alone.

So please take a deep breath, turn the page, and let's begin this journey together. With an open heart and a willingness to learn, you can create a brighter future for yourself and your children. Let's show the world that divorce doesn't have to define us—that with compassion, resilience, and guidance, we can raise happy, healthy children, no matter what our family structure looks like."

CHAPTER 1

Understanding the Emotional Landscape

Sitting across from my daughter at the breakfast table, I noticed she was unusually quiet. Her cereal was untouched, and her eyes were fixed on the swirling patterns the milk made as it slowly circled her spoon. It struck me how much this mirrored the emotional turbulence we were both experiencing after the divorce. For children, this can be a time of great confusion and upheaval. They might not have the words to express their feelings, or perhaps they don't fully understand them. It's crucial for us, as parents and caregivers, to recognize these silent signals and provide the support they need to navigate their emotions. This chapter aims to do just that—help you understand the emotional landscape your child is traversing and equip you with the tools to guide them through it.

Author: Daniel McMahon

Decoding Children's Emotional Responses to Divorce

Children are like emotional sponges, absorbing the tensions and changes brought on by divorce in ways that might surprise you. Depending on their age and personality, they can react with sadness, anger, confusion, or relief. Each of these emotions can manifest in various behaviors. For some, it might mean becoming withdrawn, retreating into a world where they feel safe. Others might act out, testing boundaries to assert some control in a situation where they have little say. You might notice your once independent child becoming clingy, seeking reassurance that they are still loved and secure. Anger is another common reaction, sometimes directed at one or both parents. This can be especially true if the child feels caught in the middle or overhears arguments not meant for their ears.

Recognizing when your child struggles emotionally is the first step in offering the support they need. Look for signs like nightmares or disturbed sleep patterns, which can indicate underlying anxiety or fear. An unexpected decline in academic performance or a loss of interest in activities they once enjoyed might also be red flags. These are not just behavioral issues; they are cries for help, signals that your child needs guidance to process their feelings. When my son started having trouble sleeping, it was a wake-up call for me to pay closer attention and start more open conversations about what was happening inside his head.

Normalizing these emotional responses is vital. Children must know that feeling sad, angry, or confused is okay. Validating their feelings helps build a foundation of trust and security. This can be as simple as sitting down with them and saying, "I know things are different now, and it's okay to feel upset about it." Encouraging them to express themselves through open-ended questions invites them to share their inner world with you. Statements like

"Tell me more about how you're feeling" or "What is making you feel this way?" can open the door to deeper understanding and connection.
Creating a safe space for these conversations is crucial. Consider setting aside time for family meetings where everyone can voice their thoughts and feelings. This gives children a structured opportunity to speak and shows them that their opinions matter. Use age-appropriate language to ensure they understand what's happening without feeling overwhelmed. It's essential to be patient and listen actively, showing empathy and understanding even when their emotions seem irrational or misplaced.

Interactive Element: Emotional Check-In

Consider using an emotional check-in at the end of each day. Ask your child to rate their feelings on a scale from one to ten or use a simple emoji chart if they're younger. This not only encourages them to reflect on their day but also provides you with valuable insights into their emotional state. It's a small step that can lead to meaningful conversations and a deeper connection.

As parents and caregivers, our role is to guide and walk alongside them, showing them that while the landscape may be unfamiliar, they are not alone. Each child's emotional response is unique, shaped by their personality and circumstances. Still, with patience, empathy, and the right tools, we can help them navigate the changes with resilience and hope.

Building an Emotional Toolbox for Kids

When it comes to helping our children navigate the emotional waves of divorce, equipping them with a robust emotional toolbox is invaluable. Think of it as giving them the tools to build resilience and understanding. For example, we might tackle a household project with a trusty hammer and nails. Still, children need emotional tools to handle life's challenges. One of the most effective tools is teaching them healthy ways to express and process their emotions.

Journaling, for example, provides a private outlet for kids to articulate their thoughts and feelings. Drawing offers a similar benefit, allowing them to express complex emotions through art, a language often more natural to children than words. These activities can become daily rituals, offering a moment of reflection and release.

Breathing exercises are another powerful addition to their toolkit. Teaching children to take slow, deliberate breaths can help them calm down and refocus when emotions run high. It's about giving them a moment to pause and center themselves, much like a reset button for their emotional state. For younger children, you might turn this into a game, asking them to imagine they are blowing up a big balloon with each breath. The visual and tactile elements make it engaging and memorable.

Language is crucial to understanding emotions, and introducing an emotional vocabulary plays a significant role here. Helping children label their feelings accurately can be empowering. It's similar to providing a map; they can navigate it more effectively once they can name their feelings. Consider using emotion cards, each depicting a different feeling with a corresponding facial expression. This visual aid can be a fun, interactive way to expand their emotional lexicon and make conversations about feelings more accessible.

Mindfulness techniques are another cornerstone of this emotional toolbox. With practices like guided imagery, children can learn to visualize calming scenarios, like walking through a peaceful forest or floating on a soft cloud. These exercises can transport them to tranquillity, even for a few moments. A game called "Five Senses" can enhance their awareness by encouraging them to notice what they can see, hear, smell, taste, and touch around them. It's about staying present, grounding them in the moment rather than being swept away by their emotions.

Consistency provides a solid foundation in a world that may feel uncertain to a child. Establishing a predictable daily schedule can offer a sense of stability and security. Whether it's a morning routine that starts with breakfast and ends with a short family walk or evening rituals that include a bedtime story and a recap of the day, these structures can be soothing. They let children know what to expect, reducing anxiety and promoting a sense of normalcy.

Visual Element: Emotion Cards

Create a set of emotion cards with your child. Use index cards, draw a face, and express different emotions on each one. Label them with words like "happy," "sad," "angry," "scared," or "excited." Spend time looking at each card together, discussing when they might feel each emotion. This can be a fun craft project and a valuable learning tool.

Family traditions post-divorce can also play a pivotal role in providing emotional stability. New rituals, like a monthly family movie night or a weekly pizza-making session, can strengthen bonds and create positive associations. These are opportunities to connect, share, and build new memories together. They remind children that while some things have changed, the essence of the family remains intact.

Integrating these strategies into your daily life helps your child cope and gives them the skills to thrive. These tools empower children to understand and manage their emotions, fostering resilience that will serve them well beyond their immediate challenges.

Recognizing and Addressing Guilt in Children

Children can internalize the world around them, often making connections that aren't there. When parents argue, even over something as trivial as the dishes left in the sink, children can misinterpret these tensions as their fault. This sense of guilt, unfounded as it may be, can weigh heavily on their young shoulders. They might think, "If only I had been better behaved," or "Maybe if I had gotten better grades, this wouldn't have happened." These thoughts can lead to a pervasive sense of responsibility for the divorce, further complicating their emotional landscape.

We must be intentional with our words and actions to counteract this misplaced guilt. Consistent reassurance is key. Let your child know repeatedly that the divorce is an adult issue stemming from problems between the parents, not because of anything the child did or didn't do. Use clear, gentle language to affirm that both parents love them unconditionally and that the changes happening do not reflect their worth or actions. Reassurance can come in many forms—verbal affirmations, reassuring hugs, and quality time spent together. Sometimes, sharing stories can help too.

Children relate well to narratives, so consider crafting stories that illustrate scenarios of non-blame. Perhaps tell them about a fictional family where the parents decide to live apart, emphasizing how the children's actions never influenced that decision. Creating a supportive narrative can significantly impact a child's understanding of the divorce.

Use metaphors or analogies that make sense to them. For instance, explain that just like sometimes friends grow apart because they change, sometimes parents do too. This doesn't mean they love their children any less. It's like when a favorite TV show ends; it's sad, but it doesn't mean the story wasn't good. By framing the situation in ways they can grasp, you paint a picture that separates them from the cause of the divorce, alleviating the burden of guilt.

Even with these efforts, staying vigilant for lingering guilt is crucial. Children often express unresolved feelings through behavior rather than words. Watch for signs such as a sudden loss of interest in previously enjoyed activities, a reluctance to engage with peers, or increased self-critical comments. These can all be red flags indicating that guilt still lingers. If you notice these cues, it may be time to revisit conversations about the divorce and reaffirm that it is not their fault. Open dialogue remains essential, as does the willingness to seek external support if needed. Sometimes, a counselor or therapist can provide a safe space for children to explore and dismantle these feelings of guilt.

Textual Element: Case Study Reflection

Consider this example: a mother noticed her son became unusually withdrawn after the divorce, often blaming himself for his parents' separation. She decided to initiate a weekly storytelling night where they would invent tales about families and adventures. Through these stories, she wove in themes of love and change that had nothing to do with the children's actions.

Over time, her son began to open up, asking questions and expressing his fears, which allowed her to reassure him directly. This approach not only helped reduce his guilt but also strengthened their bond. In addressing guilt, remember that patience and consistency are your allies. Children need time to process their emotions and accept their new reality. By maintaining open communication and providing continuous reassurance, you can help them release this burden.

Tailoring Emotional Support for Different Ages

As we navigate the labyrinth of post-divorce parenting, one truth stands out: no two children experience this transition similarly. Their reactions are as varied as the colors of a sunset, shaped by their age, personality, and even their understanding of the world. This variety necessitates a tailored approach to emotional support that respects their unique developmental stage. For our littlest ones—toddlers—play becomes a language of its own. It's in the building blocks and the make-believe tea parties where they express what they can't quite put into words. At this stage, a game of peek-a-boo or a simple puppet show can open pathways to understanding and comforting what's in their hearts. Through play, they learn about trust and consistency, crucial elements when their world seems to have shifted beneath their tiny feet.

As children grow into school age, their world becomes more logical, and so must our explanations. They're naturally curious, asking questions that sometimes catch us off guard. It's important to answer honestly but to provide just enough information to satisfy their need to understand without overwhelming them. For instance, explaining divorce as two people deciding to live in different houses because it makes them happier can be enough. This age is about balancing truth with reassurance, guiding them gently through their inquiries. They're starting to see the world in black and white, and our job is to help them navigate the grey areas with confidence and clarity.

Then comes the teenage years, when autonomy becomes a dominant theme. Adolescents are forging their identities, testing boundaries, and seeking independence. They crave respect and the opportunity to contribute to family decisions, even as they sometimes push against the limits we set. Encouraging this autonomy while still offering guidance is a delicate dance. It involves more complex discussions, allowing them to express their thoughts and feelings freely. This might mean discussing how family changes impact their social life or how they view relationships. It's a time for nuanced conversations, where listening becomes as essential as speaking.

Our approach to these age-specific needs can be enriched by understanding psychological principles. Erik Erikson, a renowned psychologist, outlined stages of psychosocial development, each marked by a central conflict. For young children, it's about building trust; for adolescents, it's crafting an identity. Jean Piaget's theory of cognitive development offers further insight, highlighting how children's thinking evolves from concrete to abstract. These frameworks remind us that children's needs are not static; they shift and grow just as they do. We can offer more effective guidance by aligning our support with these stages.

Involving children in collaborative problem-solving can empower them, giving them a sense of agency when they might otherwise feel powerless. Family meetings can serve as a platform for brainstorming solutions to shared challenges, whether deciding on a new holiday tradition or resolving sibling disputes.

These discussions teach valuable skills like negotiation and compromise and reinforce the idea that their voice matters. Encouraging children to voice their preferences helps them feel valued and respected, fostering a sense of belonging and security.

Understanding the nuances of these developmental stages allows us, as parents and caregivers, to tailor our support to meet our children's evolving needs. It's about creating an environment where they feel seen, heard, and supported, no matter where they are on their path to adulthood. This tailored support, grounded in empathy and informed by psychological insights, can make all the difference in helping children navigate the complexities of family change with grace and resilience.

The ever-changing landscape of parenting after divorce can feel challenging and uncertain. Yet, with understanding and patience, we can offer our children a steady hand as they navigate their emotions. By tailoring our support to their unique developmental needs, we help them adapt to their new family dynamics and equip them with the skills and confidence to face future challenges. This journey, while daunting, is also an opportunity to nurture resilience and foster deeper connections with those we love most.

Author: Daniel McMahon

CHAPTER 2

Effective Co-Parenting Communication

Communication with your ex-partner often becomes a complicated dance in the whirlwind of changes that divorce brings. Imagine this: you're at a school event for your child, and both you and your ex are there, standing on opposite sides of the room, unsure of how to interact. It can feel like walking on eggshells, yet finding a way to communicate effectively is crucial for your child's well-being. Clear communication can transform this awkwardness into a collaboration supporting your child's growth and happiness. The goal isn't to rekindle a relationship but to forge a new partnership focused on co-parenting.

Crafting a communication plan with your ex is one of the most foundational steps you can take. It starts with choosing the proper channels for regular updates. Text messaging is an excellent tool for quick exchanges—consider it the digital equivalent of a passing note in class. It's effective when you must confirm a pick-up time or check in about an after-school activity.

For deeper discussions, like planning for a child's upcoming surgery or deciding on a new school, scheduled phone calls are more appropriate. Setting aside specific times to talk can prevent misunderstandings in rushed or impromptu conversations. Email serves as the official channel for detailed correspondence. It's where you can document decisions or agreements, providing a written record that's easy to reference later.

Defining boundaries and expectations is equally important in maintaining a peaceful co-parenting relationship. Agree on message response times and decide which topics necessitate face-to-face discussions. Handling emotional issues in person is best while logistical details remain digital. This clarity helps prevent conflicts and ensures that both parties are on the same page. Establishing these guidelines early on sets the tone for respectful and productive communication.

Keeping the conversation child-focused is vital. Shifting the dialogue to center around your child's needs and schedules can help maintain a positive tone. Consider implementing weekly agenda meetings to discuss your child's activities and upcoming events. This creates a structured time to address logistical details, ensuring both parents are informed and involved.

A shared digital calendar can be a lifesaver here. Tools like Google Calendar allow both parents to access and update schedules in real-time, reducing the chance of missed appointments or double-booked weekends. Technology becomes an ally, not a point of contention, bridging gaps and synchronizing efforts. Addressing disagreements proactively is another cornerstone of effective co-parenting.

Develop a conflict management protocol that you both agree on for when disputes arise. This might involve pre-agreed mediators or counselors who can step in as neutral parties to help resolve issues. This framework can prevent minor disagreements from escalating into more significant conflicts. Additionally, maintaining a communication journal to document discussions can be beneficial. It serves as a record of agreements and a tool for reflection, helping both parents track progress and revisit past decisions when necessary.

Interactive Element: Communication Journal Template

Create a simple communication journal with sections for the date, topics discussed, agreements made, and any unresolved issues. Use this as a reference for future discussions, ensuring continuity and clarity.

Ultimately, the key to effective communication lies in the willingness to put aside personal grievances for the sake of your child. This isn't always easy, but it's crucial. Remember, the goal is to create a supportive environment where your child can thrive, knowing they have two parents who, despite their differences, are united in their love and care.

Navigating Difficult Conversations with Empathy

Picture this: you're sitting across from your ex at a coffee shop, trying to discuss your child's upcoming school play. The tension is palpable, and it feels like every word is a potential landmine. In moments like this, empathy becomes your best ally. Approaching conversations with compassion doesn't mean ignoring your own needs—it means recognizing the humanity in each other. Start by practicing active listening, a technique that can transform a tense exchange into a productive dialogue. When your ex speaks, really listen.

Nod your head, maintain eye contact, and occasionally paraphrase what they've said to show you're engaged. This isn't just for their benefit; it helps you understand their perspective, even if you disagree. "So, what I hear you saying is…" can be a powerful way to validate their feelings, even if the conversation remains difficult.

Reflective statements are another tool in your empathetic toolkit. These statements acknowledge the emotions behind the words, helping to diffuse tension and build a bridge of understanding. Imagine saying, "I understand how frustrating it must be to juggle work and our child's schedule," instead of jumping straight into problem-solving mode. Reflective statements don't mean you're conceding a point; they show that you're willing to understand the emotional backdrop of the discussion. This can shift the tone from adversarial to collaborative, opening the door for more constructive exchanges.

Using 'I' statements is a simple yet effective way to express your feelings without assigning blame. Instead of saying, "You never listen to me," try, "I feel unheard when we can't find a resolution." These statements focus on your experiences and needs, reducing defensiveness and paving the way for a more open dialogue. Similarly, saying, "I need us to agree about the holidays," is less confrontational than, "You always make the holidays difficult." 'I' statements allow you to communicate your needs clearly, setting the stage for mutual understanding and problem-solving.

Sometimes, conversations heat up, and emotions threaten to take over. Practicing patience and taking a pause can be crucial for maintaining composure. If you find yourself getting overwhelmed, suggest a scheduled time-out. This isn't about walking away but creating space to cool down and gather your thoughts. Agree on a time to reconvene, allowing both parties to reflect without the pressure of immediacy. During this pause, breathing exercises can be incredibly grounding. Take slow, deep breaths, focusing on the air filling your lungs and releasing it. What might seem like a small thing can be transformative, clearing your mind and allowing for a more measured response when you return to the conversation.

Redirecting your focus from problems to solutions is another impactful strategy. When discussions result in complaints or past grievances, remind yourself of the bigger picture: your child's happiness and stability. Shift the conversation towards cooperative problem-solving by proposing brainstorming sessions. Invite your ex to explore possible solutions, emphasizing that you work towards a common goal.

Be open to compromise and negotiation, recognizing that flexibility is often the key to finding workable solutions. This might mean giving a little to get a little, but the payoff is a more harmonious co-parenting relationship.

Textual Element: Reflection Section

Take a moment to reflect on a recent difficult conversation with your ex. What emotions were at play? How could you apply active listening or 'I' statements to improve future dialogues? Jot down some reflections and strategies you'd like to try next time.

Navigating difficult conversations with empathy isn't about being perfect—it's about being present. It's about repeatedly showing up, intending to understand and collaborate. And while it might not always be easy, each empathetic exchange brings you one step closer to the co-parenting relationship you both want for your child.

Utilizing Technology for Seamless Co-Parenting

Co-parenting is no exception in a world where technology touches nearly every aspect of our lives. Consider this: your child has a soccer game next weekend, and you and your ex want to be there. Instead of sifting through a flurry of texts or emails to confirm the details, co-parenting apps can streamline the process and keep everyone informed. Apps like Our Family Wizard have become a staple for many divorced parents, offering shared calendars and expense-tracking features.

With real-time updates and notifications, these tools ensure that both parents are on the same page, reducing the likelihood of miscommunication. Cozi, another popular app, helps manage family schedules and activities, making coordinating drop-offs, pick-ups, and other logistics easier. These platforms provide a space to share necessary information and foster collaboration, reminding you that you're a team working toward the same goal: your child's well-being.

While technology can be a powerful ally, it's crucial to maintain digital privacy and security, especially when sensitive family information is involved. Using secure passwords and enabling two-factor authentication can protect your accounts from unauthorized access. It's like locking the door to your virtual home. Make sure your passwords are strong and unique—think of phrases or combinations that wouldn't be easily guessed.

Two-factor authentication adds an extra layer of security, requiring verification from another device. This might seem tedious initially, but it offers peace of mind and ensures your personal information remains safe.

Shared online tools like Google Calendar and Dropbox can further enhance co-parenting coordination. Google Calendar allows parents to sync schedules, ensuring everyone knows essential dates and commitments. You can color-code events to easily differentiate between school activities, doctor appointments, and family gatherings. It's a visual representation of the shared responsibilities and commitments.

Dropbox or Google Drive, on the other hand, can be used to store and share significant documents, such as medical records, school reports, or even family photos. This centralized storage makes accessing and updating information easy, keeping everything organized and at your fingertips.

However, as wonderful as technology can be, it's essential to establish tech-free zones where family interactions take precedence over screens. Scheduled offline periods promote quality time and help maintain a healthy balance between digital and personal connections. Consider designating certain hours of the day as tech-free, where phones and devices are put aside in favor of face-to-face interactions. This could be during family dinners, where everyone can share their day or weekend mornings spent playing board games or walking. These moments create lasting memories and reinforce the idea that while technology is helpful, it should never replace genuine connection.

Visual Element: Sample Shared Calendar

Imagine a shared calendar that includes everything from school events to family trips. Color-coded entries make it easy to see who's responsible for what, and reminders ensure nothing is forgotten. It's more than just a tool; it's a visual commitment to working together for the sake of your child.

Embracing technology in your co-parenting efforts doesn't mean you must be glued to your devices. It's about using the tools available to simplify communication and coordination, allowing you to focus more on what truly matters: being present and engaged in your child's life.

Conflict Resolution Techniques for Co-Parents

Conflict in co-parenting is as common as peanut butter and jelly, but it doesn't have to be sticky. Recognizing where these conflicts stem from is the first step in untangling them. Financial disagreements often top the list. You may be debating who should cover the costs for extracurricular activities, or perhaps there's tension over shared expenses like school supplies or medical bills. Money, or the lack thereof, can stir emotions and lead to heated exchanges. Differing parenting styles are another common trigger. One parent might be more lenient, while the other prefers structure and discipline, leading to mixed messages for your child. Understanding these underlying issues provides a more straightforward path to addressing them.

When conflicts do arise, structured mediation can be a game-changer. A professional third-party mediator can provide a neutral perspective and help keep discussions on track. The mediator's role isn't to take sides but to guide both parties toward a mutually agreeable solution. Mediation sessions typically follow a structured format, beginning with each parent expressing their concerns in a safe, respectful environment.

The mediator then facilitates a discussion, encouraging both parties to explore possible solutions and compromises. This structured approach helps resolve the immediate conflict and builds skills for future disagreements.

Encouraging flexible thinking is another key aspect of conflict resolution. It's about shifting your mindset from rigid positions to more adaptable ones. Role-playing scenarios can be a fun and effective way to practice this flexibility. By stepping into each other's shoes, you can gain insights into the other parent's perspective, fostering empathy and understanding. "What if" exercises are also helpful. By exploring alternative outcomes, you can open up new possibilities and pathways for resolution. These exercises help break down barriers and encourage creative problem-solving, moving beyond entrenched positions.

A cooperative mindset is essential for effective conflict resolution. Co-parenting isn't a solo act; it's a duet that requires harmony and teamwork. Promoting a team-oriented approach to problem-solving can transform adversarial interactions into collaborative ones. Joint goal-setting activities help align parents' priorities and establish a shared vision for their child's well-being. Use visual aids like flowcharts or diagrams to map solutions and action steps. This clarifies the path forward and reinforces the concept of working together toward a common goal.

Author: Daniel McMahon

Visual Element: Conflict Resolution Flowchart

Imagine a flowchart that outlines the steps to take when a conflict arises, with branches for various scenarios and potential outcomes. Each step reminds you of your shared commitment to your child's happiness, providing a roadmap for resolving disputes with clarity and cooperation.

By embracing these techniques, you're not just resolving conflicts but modeling positive problem-solving skills for your child. Each resolution strengthens the co-parenting partnership and reinforces the idea that, despite your differences, both parents are committed to their child's best interests. As you continue to navigate the complexities of co-parenting, remember that each challenge is an opportunity to grow, learn, and build a more harmonious family dynamic.

In the next chapter, we'll explore the Legal Navigation Simplified approach, which benefits you and your ex and provides a stable environment for your children to thrive.

CHAPTER 3

Legal Navigation Simplified

I magine, if you will, standing in a courtroom, the weight of your child's future pressing heavily on your shoulders. The judge sits poised, ready to make life-altering decisions about custody—decisions that will ripple through the rest of your child's life. It's an intimidating scenario, yet it's one many of us have to face. Understanding custody agreements can make this daunting process more manageable, giving you the confidence to advocate for what's best for your child.

Custody arrangements can seem like a bewildering maze of legal jargon, but breaking them down can help. At their core, custody agreements are about deciding who decides for your child and where your child will live. Legal custody involves the authority to make substantial decisions about your child's life, like education, healthcare, and religious upbringing.

You might have joint legal custody, where both parents share these decision-making powers, or sole legal custody, where one parent holds all the authority. On the other hand, physical custody refers to where your child lives.

Joint physical custody usually means your child splits time between both parent's homes. In contrast, sole physical custody means your child primarily resides with one parent, with the other having visitation rights. Understanding these distinctions lets you see how each setup could shape your child's daily life and long-term well-being.

When courts decide custody, they consider various factors, always considering the child's best interests. Your child's age and specific needs play a significant role. Younger children might benefit from more frequent, shorter visits with each parent, while older children might handle longer stays. The court also examines each parent's ability to provide a stable environment, considering factors like the home's suitability, mental and physical health, and even the child's requests, depending on their age and maturity. These criteria ensure the custody arrangement supports your child's happiness and development.

Life, however, is anything but static, and custody agreements may need adjustments as circumstances change. Perhaps you're moving to a new city, or your child's needs have evolved due to health or educational reasons. Custody agreements are not set in stone and can be modified if both parents settle for the changes or if a significant change in circumstances occurs. Courts are generally receptive to modifications that serve the child's best interests, reflecting the understanding that as life changes, so too might the ideal living arrangement for your child.

Drafting a parenting plan can be an empowering step in creating a structured and positive co-parenting relationship. A well-thought-out plan details visitation schedules, considering weekday and weekend arrangements and holiday and vacation time. This specificity helps prevent misunderstandings and ensures you and your co-parent align your expectations. Include provisions for special occasions like birthdays or significant family events, ensuring your child maintains strong bonds with both sides of the family. A comprehensive parenting plan also considers how decisions will be made, laying out a process for resolving possible disagreements.

Interactive Element: Parenting Plan Checklist

Consider creating a checklist to assist you in drafting a thorough parenting plan. List key areas like visitation schedules, decision-making processes, and communication protocols. Regularly review and update this checklist to reflect changes in your circumstances or your child's needs.

Navigating the legal landscape of custody agreements requires patience, understanding, and a willingness to engage in open dialogue with your co-parent. By arming yourself with knowledge and preparing thoughtfully, you can make a groundwork that supports your child's growth and happiness.

Author: Daniel McMahon

Choosing the Right Legal Representation

When diving into family law, the importance of having the proper legal representation cannot be overstated. Picture this: you're amid a heated debate about custody arrangements and don't know how to turn. This is where a skilled lawyer steps in. An ideal lawyer should have deep experience in family law, which includes learning the ins and outs of custody battles, divorce settlements, and everything in between. Their familiarity with similar cases can be a game-changer. Beyond experience, strong negotiation skills are crucial. A lawyer who can advocate fiercely yet diplomatically for your interests can help secure the best outcomes for your family.

Finding the right lawyer is like searching for a needle in a haystack. Still, a structured approach can simplify the process. Start by preparing a checklist for initial consultations. Ask about their specific experience with cases like yours. How long have they practiced family law? What's their success rate in similar custody cases? These questions can provide insight into their competence and style. It's also wise to check references and past case outcomes. Please avoid asking for client testimonials or case studies illustrating their approach and effectiveness.

Understanding fee structures is another crucial step. Legal fees can quickly add up, so knowing what you're getting into is essential. Lawyers might charge flat fees for specific services, offering predictability in costs. Others work hourly, which can vary widely depending on the complexity of your case and the time it takes. Be sure to discuss retainer agreements, like down payments for services, and clarify any extra charges you might incur. This transparency helps prevent nasty surprises when the bill arrives.

Beyond traditional representation, consider exploring alternative options like collaborative law or legal consultants, which can be particularly beneficial in amicable divorces. Collaborative law involves both parties working with their lawyers and other professionals to settle without going to court. It's a team effort focused on cooperation and mutual respect, often resulting in quicker, less adversarial resolutions. Legal consultants, on the other hand, offer guidance on specific issues without full representation, which can be a cost-effective choice if you're confident handling some aspects of the process yourself.

Textual Element: Lawyer Evaluation Checklist

Here's a handy checklist for evaluating potential lawyers:

1. Experience: Years practicing family law? Success stories in similar cases?

2. Negotiation: How do they handle conflict? Examples of successful talks?

3. References: Can they provide client testimonials?

4. Fees: Detailed explanation of billing methods and any potential extra costs.

Each tick on this list gets you closer to finding a lawyer who understands the law and your unique situation.

Author: Daniel McMahon

Preparing for Court: What to Expect

Walking into a courtroom can feel like stepping onto a stage, with roles to play and scripts to follow. Understanding the process can ease some of the anxiety. It all begins with the initial filings. This is where you submit your divorce petition, laying out your requests for custody, support, and division of assets. Your ex will be able to respond, setting the stage for proceedings. Deadlines are crucial here; missing them can delay your case.

Once the initial paperwork is sorted, you enter the discovery phase. This involves gathering evidence, like financial records and communication logs, to support your claims. Both parties exchange this information, ensuring transparency. It's a time of preparation and, often, negotiation as you work to present a clear picture of your situation to the court.

Courtroom etiquette is more than just a set of rules—it's about respecting the process and those involved. Dressing appropriately is the first step. Think business attire: suits, dresses, or anything that conveys seriousness. Leave the jeans and sneakers at home. Punctuality is equally essential; arriving late can reflect poorly on your commitment to the case. When addressing the judge, use "Your Honor" to convey respect. Speak clearly and truthfully, whether answering questions or presenting your case. Interaction with opposing counsel requires politeness, even if tensions run high. Remember, the courtroom is a formal environment; maintaining decorum can positively influence the proceedings.

Preparation is your ally in court, and proper documents are key. Financial affidavits are essential, detailing your income, expenses, and assets. These give the court a clear financial snapshot for support and asset division decisions. Asset inventories list valuable items, from real estate to bank accounts. Don't overlook communication records, especially if they illustrate agreements or conflicts with your ex. Emails, text messages, and written agreements can all be relevant. Organizing these documents before your court date will help you present a well-structured case, reducing the risk of fumbling or forgetting important details.

Managing the emotional toll of court proceedings is as important as managing the legal aspects. Court days can be stressful, and it's easy to feel overwhelmed. Stress management techniques, like deep breathing or visualization, can help calm your nerves. Imagine yourself in a peaceful place, or take slow, deep breaths before entering the courtroom. Maintaining composure is crucial, even if the proceedings become heated. Focus on the facts, not the emotions, and remember your goals. Personal grievances make it easy to get sidetracked, but staying centered on what's best for your child can provide clarity amidst chaos. Sometimes, having a stress ball or a comforting item in your pocket can help ground you during tense moments.

The courtroom can be frightening, but you can navigate it confidently with preparation and composure. Keep your focus on the outcome you desire and trust in the process. Remember, every step you take is towards creating a stable, loving environment for your child.

Author: Daniel McMahon

Mediation: A Path to Amicable Agreements

Imagine sitting across the table from your ex, not in a courtroom but in a more relaxed setting, to reach an understanding rather than fighting a battle. Mediation offers this opportunity. It's a process where a neutral mediator helps both parties discuss and resolve their disputes outside of court. In dissimilar litigation, where a judge makes the final decision, mediation empowers you and your ex to find solutions that work for both of you. The mediator acts as a facilitator, controlling the conversation and ensuring both voices are heard. This process is voluntary, meaning both parties must agree to participate. One of its greatest strengths is confidentiality; discussions in mediation aren't part of the public record, allowing for more open and honest communication.

The benefits of mediation extend beyond its simplicity. It's often more cost-effective than traditional litigation, making it an attractive option for many families. Reducing legal fees means more resources can be allocated towards your children's needs rather than legal battles. Mediation also helps preserve amicable relationships. By focusing on collaboration rather than conflict, it encourages respect and understanding. This can primarily benefit co-parenting, setting a foundation for future interactions. The process is less adversarial, reducing stress and fostering cooperation that can help everyone involved.

To make the most of mediation, preparation is key. Start by setting realistic goals and priorities. What are the most critical issues you want to resolve? A clear understanding of your objectives will keep the discussions focused and productive. Prioritize the well-being of your children and think about how each decision will impact their lives.

Effective communication is crucial during mediation. Practice active listening, which involves giving your full attention to your ex's perspective before responding. This shows respect and can lead to more constructive discussions. Be open to compromise, as successful mediation often requires finding a middle ground. Remember, the aim is to reach an agreement that benefits everyone, particularly your children.

Once you've reached a consensus, it's time to draft a mediation agreement. This document outlines the outcomes of your discussions and serves as a legally binding agreement. Key elements include details about custody arrangements, visitation schedules, and any financial agreements regarding child support or shared expenses. Clarity is crucial; ensure the terms are specific to avoid misunderstandings later. Both parties should review the agreement thoroughly, ideally with legal counsel, to ensure it meets legal standards and is enforceable.

Visual Element: Sample Mediation Agreement Template

Creating a mediation agreement can be daunting, but a template simplifies the process. Start with sections for custody arrangements, visitation schedules, and financial contracts. Leave space for both parents to sign, acknowledging their commitment to the terms. This template covers all necessary details, providing a solid foundation for your co-parenting relationship.

Author: Daniel McMahon

By choosing mediation, you're opting for a path prioritizing harmony and collaboration, setting the stage for a positive co-parenting experience. This approach benefits you and your ex and provides a stable environment for your children to thrive. As you continue exploring the legal aspects of divorce, remember that mediation offers a way to resolve conflicts amicably, with the well-being of your family at its heart.

CHAPTER 4

Financial Stability After Divorce

Picture this: You've just arrived home after a long day. The kids are settled, and you have a moment to yourself. Maybe you're grappling with bills on the kitchen table, each a reminder of the financial shifts that have come with your new reality. Navigating finances post-divorce can feel like piecing together a puzzle. But here's the thing—you're not alone in this. Many of us find ourselves in similar shoes, trying to balance our bank accounts while balancing our lives. The good news? With some planning, you can create a financial roadmap that keeps you afloat and sets you on a path toward stability and peace of mind.

Let's start by assessing where you stand financially. This means closely examining your income, expenses, and assets. Begin by listing all your sources of revenue. This includes your salary, alimony child support, and side gigs or investments. Knowing exactly what's coming in each month is crucial. Next, categorize your expenses. Break them into fixed costs like mortgage or rent and variable expenses like groceries or entertainment.

This precise categorization helps you see where your money goes and highlights areas where you might cut back. Don't forget to inventory your assets as well. This includes everything from your car to any savings accounts. A complete picture of your financial landscape lets you make informed decisions.

Once you've got a handle on your current situation, it's time to set some realistic financial goals. Start with short-term targets like minimizing debt. You could pay off credit card balances or build up a small emergency fund within a year. These goals provide immediate direction and motivation. Then, think long-term. Consider bigger ambitions, such as saving for your children's education. You can contribute to a college fund or set aside money for their future endeavors. These goals might feel daunting, but laying the groundwork early makes them more achievable.

Developing a comprehensive budget is your next step. Think of it as your financial blueprint. Begin with a template—it can be as simple as a spreadsheet or a dedicated budgeting app. Allocate funds for essential categories like housing, food, and savings. Make sure your budget reflects your new financial realities post-divorce. Some categories might need more attention than before, while others could be scaled back. Regularly revisiting your budget helps keep you on track and allows for adjustments. It's a living document, evolving with your circumstances.

In today's digital age, budgeting apps can be a lifesaver. Apps like Mint offer a user-friendly platform to track both savings and spending. Imagine having all your financial information in one place, accessible with just a tap. These apps often feature pie charts for a glance at your weekly expenditures, helping you visualize where your money goes. You can even manage bill payments, credit cards, and investments in one app.

You Need A Budget is another excellent option. It helps you stick to spending plans and offers strategies for reducing debt. Though it has a monthly fee, many find the financial insights it provides worth the cost.

These tools simplify financial management, offering alerts for overspending and personalized tips to help stretch your dollar further. While they come with a learning curve, their potential to streamline your financial life is immense. Plus, many offer free trials to determine which best fits your needs. By including these tools in your routine, you can gain clarity and control over your finances, turning what was once a source of stress into a manageable part of your life.

Embracing these strategies and tools can transform your financial landscape, making it possible to build a stable future for you and your family.

Managing Child Support Effectively

Navigating child support can feel like deciphering a foreign language. Yet, understanding how it's calculated and what it covers can make the process smoother. Each state has its formula, often constructed based on the non-custodial parent's income and the number of children involved. This formula ensures kids receive a fair share of financial support. For example, New York uses percentages: 17% of the non-custodial parent's income for one child, 25% for two, and so on. It's important to know what child support is meant to cover.

Typically, this includes basic needs like food, shelter, and clothing. Still, it can also extend to healthcare, education, and even childcare expenses. Understanding these guidelines helps you see where the money should go, ensuring it directly benefits your child.

Timely child support payments are crucial for maintaining stability in your child's life. Setting up automatic bank transfers is one effective strategy to ensure payments are never late. This way, the money arrives like clockwork without any stress or oversight. If payments become inconsistent, there are legal avenues you can pursue to enforce them. These include wage garnishment or even legal action, though it's always best to try and resolve issues amicably first. Ensuring these payments come through regularly is not just about meeting legal obligations; it's about providing your child with the security they deserve.

Once the funds arrive, using them wisely is key. Prioritize expenses that directly impact your child's well-being and development. Education-related costs are often at the top of this list. Whether it's school supplies or fees for extracurricular activities, these investments in your child's future can make a significant difference. Extracurriculars, in particular, offer opportunities for growth and socialization, helping your child build skills and confidence. These experiences can be invaluable, providing both immediate joy and long-term benefits.

As time goes by, it's essential to remain flexible and prepared for changes in child support needs. Kids grow, and so do their expenses. Educational costs may increase as they advance in school, and new interests might lead to additional extracurricular fees.

Health-related expenses can also shift, especially as children hit growth spurts or need braces or other medical care. Anticipating these changes means you won't be caught off guard. Planning can involve supporting these evolving needs, ensuring you have a cushion when new expenses arise.

Child support is not just a financial transaction; it's a commitment to your child's future. It requires active management and planning to ensure the resources are used effectively and adapt to changing circumstances. By understanding the guidelines, ensuring payments are consistent, and wisely allocating funds, you create a stable environment for your child to thrive.

Financial Planning for Two Households

Managing finances across two households might feel like juggling flaming torches. Still, with the right strategies, it becomes much more manageable. One of the first things to tackle is identifying and dividing shared financial responsibilities. This can include expenses like healthcare, where agreeing on who covers what is crucial. One parent handles the monthly premiums, while the other handles the co-pays. Similarly, school fees should be coordinated.

Whether it's tuition, uniforms, or extracurricular costs, having a clear plan ensures these responsibilities don't slip through the cracks. Clear communication about these shared costs can prevent misunderstandings and ensure both households contribute to the children's needs.

Optimizing resource allocation is another important aspect of financial planning. With two households, it's easy to buy double of everything. Instead, consider combining shopping lists with your ex to buy in bulk. Items like toiletries and non-perishable foods are often cheaper when purchased in larger quantities. Not only does this save money, but it also reduces waste.

Additionally, consider what can be shared or repurposed for larger purchases like electronics or furniture. The gaming console or TV can travel with the kids between homes, or a piece of furniture can rotate based on need. This approach maximizes resources and fosters a sense of continuity for the children as they transition between homes.

Navigating tax implications is another critical component of financial planning post-divorce. Filing status changes, such as moving to the head of household, can have significant tax benefits, including a higher standard deduction. Determining who claims the children as dependents can also impact tax credits and deductions, like the Earned Income Tax Credit. If both parents alternate claiming the children, it's essential to ensure this is clearly outlined and agreed upon to avoid complications come tax season. Understanding these nuances can make a substantial difference in your financial outlook, so it might be worth consulting a tax professional to guide you through these considerations.

Exploring financial assistance programs can provide a vital safety net, especially for single parents. Government assistance programs often base eligibility on income and family size, offering healthcare, food, and housing support. It's worth researching what's available in your state and applying for programs to ease your financial burden. Community resources are another avenue to consider. Many local organizations offer financial aid, educational workshops, or food banks to support needy families. Connecting with these resources can provide additional support and help stretch your budget further, ensuring that both households can maintain stability and comfort.

While managing two households, it's easy to feel overwhelmed by the financial strain. But remember, you're not alone in this. Many parents have successfully navigated these waters, finding creative solutions to meet their children's needs. With careful planning, open communication, and a readiness to explore all available resources, you can create a financial plan that supports both homes and provides a stable environment for your kids during this transition.

Overcoming Financial Anxiety

Life post-divorce often feels like a rollercoaster, and financial anxiety is one of those steep drops that can take your breath away. You might lie awake at night, worrying about your financial future. Uncertainty about what's coming next can be deeply unsettling. The rising cost of living doesn't help, with everything from groceries to gas prices climbing steadily. It's easy to feel overwhelmed and unsure how to keep it together, especially when juggling so much. Recognizing these stressors is the first step toward tackling them. Identifying what triggers your anxiety explicitly can help you address it more effectively. It could be the unpredictability of income, the fear of unexpected expenses, or the pressure of maintaining two households. Pinpointing the cause can guide you in finding solutions that ease the burden.

Developing coping mechanisms is crucial to managing this financial anxiety. Stress-reducing practices like meditation or exercise can offer some relief. Even a few minutes of deep breathing or a short walk can clear your mind and help you regain perspective.

Physical activity releases endorphins, those feel-good chemicals in your brain that can lift your mood and reduce stress. Additionally, financial literacy workshops can be incredibly empowering. A better understanding of managing your finances can build confidence and reduce anxiety. These workshops often cover budgeting, saving, and investing, providing tools to help you feel more in control of your financial situation. Many of these resources are available online, making them accessible and convenient.

Engaging with a financial advisor can also be a game-changer. These professionals can offer personalized advice tailored to your unique situation. They can help you create a secure financial plan, guiding everything from retirement savings to investment strategies. Finding a trustworthy advisor is essential, someone who understands your goals and can help you achieve them. Look for someone with a solid reputation and experience working with families like yours. A good advisor will listen to your concerns, answer your questions, and work with you to develop a plan that meets your needs. They can help demystify the complexities of finance, providing peace of mind and a more straightforward path forward.

Building a financial safety net is another crucial step. An emergency fund can cushion the blow of unexpected expenses, whether it's a car repair, a medical bill, or a temporary loss of income. Start small if you need to, setting aside a little each month until it grows. Consider setting up automatic savings transfers to a dedicated account.

This way, you save without thinking about it; those contributions add up over time. This safety net can alleviate anxiety about the future, knowing you have a buffer to fall back on if needed. It's like having an umbrella ready for a rainy day, offering protection and reassurance. Facing financial anxiety head-on is about taking small, manageable steps. It's about finding ways to regain control and reduce stress, even when the road ahead seems uncertain. As you build your financial literacy, seek guidance, and create a safety net, you're not just managing anxiety—creating a foundation of stability for yourself and your children.

As we wrap up this chapter on financial stability, remember that these steps are about building a solid framework for your new life. Economic stability is within reach, even amidst the challenges. With thoughtful planning and the proper support, you're setting the stage for a more secure and confident future. Let's explore how to use this stability to foster age-specific parenting strategies that nurture your child's growth and well-being.

Author: Daniel McMahon

CHAPTER 5

Age-Specific Parenting Strategies

Imagine sitting on the floor with your young child, surrounded by a sea of colorful blocks and stuffed animals. You're trying to explain why Daddy or Mommy no longer live at home. Their big, curious eyes look up at you, filled with questions they can't quite articulate. It's a moment where your words matter more than ever, shaping their understanding of family and love. This chapter guides you through those tender conversations, helping you communicate comfortably and age-appropriately.

Communicating Divorce to Young Children

When talking to young children about divorce, simplicity is your best friend. Young kids are beginning to develop logical thinking, so complex explanations or legal jargon will likely leave them confused or anxious. Instead, use straightforward language that reflects their world. You might say, "Mommy and Daddy don't get along anymore, so we will live in different houses.

But we love you and will always take care of you." This approach helps them understand the situation without overwhelming them with adult complexities. Visual aids can be invaluable here. Picture books about families in all shapes and sizes can illustrate these changes in a way they can grasp. Stories where characters experience similar situations can normalize their feelings and provide comfort.

Reassurance is crucial. Your child needs to know that your love for them hasn't changed. Regularly remind them that both parents still love and care for them deeply. Create activities that reinforce this bond. You could have a family drawing time where everyone makes pictures of their family or create a photo album together filled with happy memories. These activities are more than just fun; they're tangible reminders of the constant love despite other changes. It's about showing them that while the family structure may look different, the love that binds you together is steadfast.

Maintaining familiar routines can also provide the stability they crave. Children thrive on predictability; keeping certain rituals unchanged can offer them a comforting sense of normalcy. If bedtime always involves a bath followed by a story, keep it that way. These nightly rituals act as anchors in their day, providing a familiar rhythm that reassures them even when other parts of their world feel uncertain. Regular playdates with friends help maintain their social connections and give a sense of continuity. These interactions remind them that, while some things have changed, much remains the same.

Young children often fear being abandoned or unloved, mainly when upheaval occurs. Address these fears directly and gently. Let them know that their feelings are normal and that it's okay to have questions about what's happening. Be patient with their questions, even if they ask the same ones repeatedly. Reassure them that both parents will always be there for them, even if they live in separate homes. This might involve explaining new living arrangements in simple, reassuring terms, helping them understand that they'll have spaces in both homes where they feel safe and loved.

Interactive Element: Storybook Activity

Create a storybook together that depicts their new family situation. Encourage your child to draw pictures and craft a narrative demonstrating love from both parents, regardless of living arrangements. This activity can help them process the changes and feel more secure.

Addressing young children's concerns about divorce requires patience, empathy, and a gentle approach. By using clear language, reinforcing love, maintaining routines, and directly addressing fears, you can help your child navigate this transition with greater security and confidence. It's all about creating a supportive environment where they feel understood, cherished, and safe as they adjust to their new normal.

Author: Daniel McMahon

Supporting Pre-Teens Through Transition

Navigating the world of pre-teens is like stepping into a bustling marketplace full of excitement, confusion, and the occasional emotional outburst. These kids are at an age where they're beginning to form their identities, and the changes brought on by divorce can feel like a whirlwind. It's a time when open dialogues become your most valuable tool. Scheduling one-on-one time with your pre-teens can help create a safe space to share their views and feelings. Start with a simple walk in the park or a quiet evening at home, where minimal distractions make them feel heard.

Please encourage them to express themselves through journaling, which can be a therapeutic outlet for those swirling emotions. Prompts like "What made me happy today?" or "What's something I'm worried about?" can guide them in unpacking their feelings, providing clarity and relief.

Building resilience and independence in pre-teens is crucial as they adapt to new family dynamics. Please encourage them to explore new activities or join clubs that pique their interest. Whether it's soccer, chess, or drama, these experiences can boost their confidence and afford a sense of belonging. Role-playing scenarios at home can be a fun way to teach problem-solving skills. You might set up a situation where they must negotiate with a sibling over shared chores or plan a family outing.

Through these exercises, they learn to think critically and develop solutions. These skills will help them well in all aspects of life. Social dynamics are another layer to consider, as divorce can ripple through your child's friendships and school interactions. Be mindful of changes in their peer relationships. They might pull away from friends or experience shifts in their social circle. Please encourage them to maintain connections by inviting friends over or planning group activities. If they face bullying or teasing, offer support and strategies to cope. Let them know it's okay to seek help from teachers or counselors if needed. You must stand by them, providing guidance and reassurance as they navigate these social waters.

Pre-adolescence is a period marked by emotional fluctuations, where mood swings can feel like a rollercoaster ride. Helping your pre-teen manage these ups and downs starts with recognizing the signs. Please pay attention to changes in their behavior, like irritability or withdrawal, which might signal underlying stress from family changes. Encourage healthy outlets for their emotions. Sports, art, or music can provide an escape and a means of expression. They may paint, lose themselves in the colors and textures, or join a local team, channeling their energy into the game. These activities help release pent-up feelings and offer a sense of accomplishment and joy.

As you support your pre-teen through this transition, remember that patience and empathy are key. They're grappling with complex emotions and challenges; your understanding can make all the difference. By fostering open communication, encouraging independence, monitoring social dynamics, and guiding them through emotional changes, you're helping them build a strong foundation for the years ahead. Your role is to guide and walk alongside them, offering a steady hand as they navigate this new chapter in their lives.

Guiding Teenagers in a Post-Divorce World

Teenagers live in a realm where autonomy reigns supreme. They're just beginning to carve out their identities, seeking independence while still needing a safety net. Balancing this newfound freedom with guidance is like walking a tightrope. It's important to set boundaries and grant them the space to grow. Creating an environment where they feel involved in decision-making processes can empower them. This could involve them in family discussions about schedules or encourage them to voice their opinions on matters directly affecting them. It's about giving them a say while ensuring they recognize the importance of responsibility and accountability.

Divorce can shake a teenager's self-esteem and self-concept to its core. They might start questioning their place in the world or doubting their self-worth. Encouraging self-expression can be a powerful antidote. Support their interests in fashion, music, or writing as outlets for expressing their identity and emotions.

Let them experiment with different styles or join creative writing groups to explore their thoughts. Providing positive reinforcement and support is crucial, too. Recognize their efforts and achievements, no matter how small. A simple "I'm proud of you" can boost their confidence and reassure them of your unwavering support during this uncertain time.

Academics and extracurricular commitments can be a lifeline for teenagers, offering structure and a sense of normalcy. As a parent, supporting these commitments is key to helping them maintain focus and momentum. Coordinate with teachers and coaches to ensure they're aware of any changes at home that might affect your teenager's performance or behavior. Being proactive in these discussions can lead to a more supportive environment for your child. Encourage their participation in school events, sports, or clubs. These activities keep them engaged and provide a healthy outlet for stress and a way to connect with peers with similar interests.

Discussing dating and relationships with your teenager can be tricky, especially when they've witnessed a marriage dissolve. It's essential to have open conversations about what healthy relationships look like. Respect, communication, and mutual support are the cornerstones of a strong relationship. Set guidelines for teen dating that reflect your values and expectations but also give them room to explore and learn. Encouraging discussions about their relationship views can help them process their feelings and develop a healthy understanding of love and partnership.

Textual Element: Reflection Section

Reflect on a recent conversation with your teenager about their autonomy. What went well? What could be improved? Jot down some thoughts and strategies for future discussions to help balance guidance and independence.

As you navigate parenting a teenager in a post-divorce world, remember that your role is to provide a steady presence. They're figuring out who and where they fit; your support is vital to that journey. By balancing autonomy with guidance, addressing self-esteem issues, supporting academic commitments, and discussing relationships, you're helping them build a strong foundation for adulthood. Your involvement and encouragement can make all the difference as they navigate these formative years.

Addressing Young Adults' Concerns

As your child ages into adulthood, their challenges can feel monumental. Transitioning from the comforts of adolescence to the responsibilities of adulthood is no small feat, especially against the backdrop of family changes. It's crucial to acknowledge the maturity they bring to conversations. Treat them as partners, valuing their insights and feelings. When discussing family finances or college plans, be transparent and inclusive. This might mean sharing the realities of tuition costs or the impact of financial aid, helping them understand the bigger picture. By involving them in these discussions, you empower them to make informed decisions about their future, fostering a sense of responsibility and ownership over their path.

Life transitions can be daunting, but young adults can confidently navigate them with your support. Whether they're moving out or starting college, your guidance is invaluable. Discuss the logistics and emotional aspects of these changes openly. Discuss budgeting for groceries or managing time between classes, work, and social commitments. These conversations prepare them for practical challenges and offer reassurance that they're not alone in facing them. Please encourage them to explore career aspirations, whether that's through internships, part-time jobs, or networking opportunities. Showing interest in their dreams affirms your support and helps them feel more secure in pursuing their passions.

Maintaining a sense of family continuity is crucial during this time. Traditions and connections offer stability and comfort even as everything else evolves. Plan regular family gatherings or trips, giving your young adult something to look forward to amidst the hustle of their new life. These moments reinforce the bonds that hold your family together, reminding them they have a home to return to no matter where they go. It's about creating memories that transcend the physical space, anchoring them in the love and support of family.

Young adults often seek to form healthy adult relationships but might need guidance navigating commitment and conflict resolution. Encourage open conversations about what makes a relationship strong and fulfilling. Share your experiences, if appropriate, highlighting the importance of communication and compromise. Encourage them to seek therapy or counseling if they encounter challenges. Professional guidance can offer insights and strategies for managing relationship dynamics, providing them with tools to build successful partnerships. It's about equipping them with the skills to form connections that enhance their lives and support their growth.

Author: Daniel McMahon

Your role as a parent shifts as your child enters adulthood, transitioning from directing their path to walking alongside them as they forge their own. By respecting their maturity, preparing them for life changes, fostering family ties, and guiding them in relationships, you help them build a solid foundation for their future. This chapter in their lives is as much about growth as it is about maintaining the love and connection that have always been there. As you continue to support them, remember that your presence and encouragement make all the difference in their journey to independence.

As we wrap up this chapter, remember that each stage of your child's life brings new challenges and opportunities. Your support and understanding are constant, helping them navigate the complexities of growing up. In the next chapter, we'll explore how building emotional resilience in children and tapping into community resources can further bolster your child's support network.

CHAPTER 6

Building Emotional Resilience in Children

Imagine a world where every child feels heard and their emotions are acknowledged and celebrated. It's a place where they can express their feelings, no matter how big or small, without fear of judgment or misunderstanding. Creating such an environment might seem daunting, but it's within reach. It starts with us, the adults in their lives, paving the way for open emotional expression.

Establishing a safe space for your child to share their emotions is like giving them a soft landing in a sometimes turbulent world. One way to do this is by designating a specific time for family check-ins. These check-ins could be once a week, over Sunday breakfast, or during a quiet evening at home. It's a time when everyone pauses to reflect on their week, to talk about what went well and what felt challenging. Having this regular touchpoint helps children know there's always a time when their voice will be heard, reinforcing the idea that their feelings matter.

Incorporating a "feelings corner" in your home can encourage emotional expression. Picture a cozy nook with comfy cushions, a few picture books, and a set of emotion cards. These cards, each depicting a different emotion with a simple word and picture, can help children identify and articulate their feelings. It's a space where they can retreat when emotions run high, offering them a moment to pause and reflect before rejoining the world. This corner becomes a sanctuary, a reminder that it's okay to feel and that they have the tools to navigate those feelings.

As parents, modeling emotional expression ourselves is a powerful way to teach our children. Sharing personal stories about how we handle our emotions can offer valuable insights. Maybe you talk about a time you felt angry and how taking a walk helped you calm down. Or you could share a moment of joy and how it made you feel more connected to those around you. Using "I feel" statements during family discussions can also demonstrate healthy communication. For example, saying, "I feel worried when the house is noisy because it's hard to think," shows children how to express emotions without blaming others, fostering an environment of understanding and empathy.

Creative outlets are another fantastic way for children to express their emotions. Drawing or painting can serve as a window into their internal world, allowing them to project and explore their feelings through art. Please set up a small art station with supplies like paper, crayons, and paints, and encourage them to create whenever they feel inspired. Music, too, is a powerful medium for expression.

Please encourage your child to develop playlists reflecting their moods or sing along to their favorite songs. Music provides an emotional release, offering children a way to process feelings that might be difficult to express in words. Helping children expand their emotional vocabulary is crucial for their development. Emotion word games can make learning fun and engaging. You might play a game where you take turns describing how a character in a book or movie might feel in a given situation.

This builds vocabulary and empathy as they consider perspectives outside their own. Storytime focusing on characters' emotions is another excellent tool. Choose books where characters experience various emotions and pause to discuss how the characters might feel and why. This practice helps children better understand and communicate their feelings, laying the foundation for strong emotional intelligence.

Interactive Element: Emotion Word Game

Create a simple emotion word game with your child. Write different emotions on cards, and take turns picking a card. Then, act out or describe a time when you felt that way. This game encourages expression and helps build emotional vocabulary.

By fostering an environment rich in opportunities for emotional expression, you help your child navigate their feelings and build their resilience. In this space, they learn that emotions are a natural part of life, and with the right tools, they can manage and understand them. You're equipping your child with the skills to face life's challenges with confidence and compassion through consistent practice and support.

Developing Coping Mechanisms for Stress

In the hustle and bustle of daily life, stress can sneak up on our children like an unexpected rainstorm. It's there before we know it, bringing with it a myriad of emotional and physical responses. Teaching kids to manage stress is like giving them an umbrella and showing them how to use it. One effective method is through breathing exercises, which can be both simple and powerful. Take "balloon breathing," for instance. Please encourage your child to imagine they are inflating a giant balloon with each deep breath and slowly deflating it as they breathe out. This visualization helps them focus their mind and calms their nervous system, making stress feel more manageable. Progressive muscle relaxation is another technique that can work wonders. Guide your child to tense and slowly release each muscle group, starting from their toes and working up to their head. This process helps them recognize where they hold tension and how to let it go. It's like a gentle reset for their body, allowing them to release built-up stress and find peace amidst the chaos.

Beyond physical techniques, fostering a problem-solving mindset can be a game-changer for children facing stress. Life is full of challenges, big and small, and teaching kids to approach these with curiosity rather than fear can empower them to take control. Try role-playing different scenarios together. You could create a story where a character faces a dilemma, and together, you brainstorm possible solutions. This practice builds their confidence, showing them they have the tools to tackle whatever comes their way. Encouraging journaling is another way to promote reflective thinking. Children can process experiences and emotions by writing about their day, gaining clarity on what stresses them and why. Journals become a safe space where they can explore their thoughts without judgment, helping them develop a deeper understanding of themselves and the world around them.

Physical activity is crucial in reducing stress, acting as a natural mood booster. Regular movement releases endorphins, those feel-good chemicals in the brain that help counteract stress. Family walks or bike rides can be an excellent way to incorporate exercise into your routine, offering physical benefits and quality time together. These outings don't have to be long or intense; even a short stroll around the block can make a difference. If your child is more interested in group activities, team sports or individual exercise classes can provide an engaging outlet for energy and stress. Whether it's soccer, dance, or martial arts, participating in organized activities helps children stay active while fostering social connections and teamwork skills.

Establishing a calming routine is another strategy that can help children manage stress. Predictability is comforting, and incorporating soothing activities into their daily schedule creates a sense of stability. Bedtime rituals, for example, can include reading a peaceful story or practicing relaxation techniques before sleep. These routines signal the brain that it's time to unwind, promoting restful sleep and a better overall mood. Afternoon "quiet time" can serve as a decompression period, allowing your child to step back from the busyness of the day. They might read, listen to calming music, or sit silently during this time. These moments of tranquillity teach children the value of slowing down and give them space to recharge.

Stress is an inevitable part of life, but by equipping children with these coping mechanisms, you're helping them build resilience. They learn to weather the storms and dance in the rain, finding joy and balance even in challenging times.

Building a Child-Centric Support Network

Imagine your child at school, surrounded by the comforting presence of their teacher or coach. These figures often become trusted allies, providing guidance and support beyond academics or sports. Teachers can be a beacon of stability, noticing when something's off or offering a listening ear when a child needs to talk. Coaches, too, play a vital role. They teach resilience and teamwork through practice and team activities, instilling life skills beyond the field. Please encourage your child to see these adults as part of their support network, people they can turn to when life feels overwhelming.

Extended family members like aunts or uncles can be invaluable in this network. They offer a different perspective, one that's rooted in family but a step removed from parental dynamics. A trusted aunt might take your child for a weekend, offering a change of scenery and an opportunity to talk in a relaxed setting. An uncle could become a mentor, sharing hobbies or skills that build confidence and self-esteem. These relationships enrich your child's life, providing a sense of continuity and family connection that's crucial during times of change.

Facilitating peer connections is another cornerstone of a robust support network. Friendships offer emotional support, providing a space where kids can be themselves without the weight of adult expectations. Organizing playdates or encouraging participation in group activities can nurture these bonds. Whether it's a weekend sleepover or joining a club at school, these interactions are vital for emotional growth. They offer a break from family stress and a chance to build a social circle that supports and understands them. Community groups, too, can be a great way to meet new friends and develop a sense of belonging.

Tapping into community resources can further bolster your child's support network. Many areas offer local support groups or workshops for children facing similar challenges. These groups provide a safe space to connect with peers who understand their experiences, fostering empathy and shared resilience. Libraries and community centers often host family programs or activities that encourage social interaction and learning. These resources offer support and enrich your child's life with new experiences and opportunities to learn.

Empowering your child to seek support is critical to building their network. Teach them that asking for help is a strength, not a weakness. Role-playing scenarios can be a practical way to make this skill. You might set up a pretend situation where they must ask a teacher for extra help or talk to a friend about a problem. Practicing these conversations in a safe, supportive environment builds confidence. Consider providing "help cards" with contact information for trusted adults, reinforcing that they have resources at their fingertips. These cards could include phone numbers for family members, teachers, or counselors, offering a tangible reminder that support is just a call away.

You create a safety net for your child by weaving together these elements. It's a network that catches them when they fall, offers guidance when they lose, and celebrates with them when they succeed. Building this support system is an ongoing process that evolves as your child grows and their needs change. The goal remains to provide a nurturing environment where they feel safe, valued, and connected.

Integrating Therapeutic Interventions

Every parent wants the best for their child, especially regarding their emotional health. Sometimes, though, our kids' challenges may require more than we, as parents, can provide alone. Recognizing when therapy might be beneficial is key. Persistent changes in mood or behavior can be a red flag. You might notice your child withdrawing from activities they once enjoyed or having trouble keeping up with daily routines. If these changes linger and affect their well-being, consider professional help. Therapy isn't a sign of failure; it's a proactive step towards supporting your child's mental health.

Finding a fit that suits your child's unique needs is essential when exploring therapeutic options. For younger children, play therapy can be particularly effective. This approach allows kids to express emotions and work through difficulties naturally and comfortably, using play as a medium for communication. It's a space where they can explore feelings without the pressure of direct conversation. Older kids might benefit from cognitive-behavioral therapy or CBT. This therapy helps them identify and change negative thought patterns, equipping them with tools to manage emotions and stress more effectively. Each therapy type offers a different pathway to healing, and sometimes, it may take trial and error to find the right match.

Working with mental health professionals is a collaborative process. It's about building a partnership that supports your child's progress. Regular updates and feedback sessions with the therapist can keep you informed and involved, allowing you to reinforce therapeutic strategies at home. These sessions provide an opportunity to discuss what's working well and what might need adjustment. Involving your child in setting therapy goals can also be empowering, giving them a sense of ownership over their journey. They're more likely to engage and benefit from the experience when they feel invested.

Helping children view therapy as a positive and proactive step is crucial. It's not about fixing something broken; it's about growing and learning. Storybooks with characters who attend therapy can be a great way to normalize the experience. These stories show children that therapy is just another tool in their toolkit, something that helps them become the best version of themselves. Discussions that frame therapy as a means for growth can further reinforce this perspective. You might say, "Therapy is like having a coach for your feelings, someone to help you understand and manage them better." This framing demystifies the process and can help remove any stigma or fear of seeking professional help.

Children who embrace therapy often find it a haven. In this place, they can explore their emotions with guidance and support. By integrating therapeutic interventions into your child's life when needed, you're addressing immediate concerns and laying the groundwork for lifelong emotional resilience. And while the decision to pursue therapy can feel daunting, remember that it's a step towards giving your child the support they need to thrive. It's about providing them the tools to navigate their emotions and challenges with confidence and strength. In its many forms, therapy can be a powerful ally in helping your child build a healthy, happy future.

In the next chapter, we'll explore blended family dynamics. Introducing a new partner to your children is a significant step in blending families and requires sensitivity and careful planning.

CHAPTER 7

Blended Family Dynamics

Imagine standing on a beach where the waves gently wash over the sand, each bringing something new and taking something old. This is what blending families can feel like—constantly shifting, bringing in new experiences, and letting go of past ones. Introducing a new partner to your children can be one of the most delicate parts of this process. It's a significant step that requires careful timing, patience, and understanding. When is the right moment to let your kids meet your new partner? This question can weigh heavily on your mind, as balancing your love life and your children's emotional readiness is crucial. Experts suggest waiting until the relationship is stable, typically around 9 to 12 months, before introducing a new partner to your children (Source 1). This waiting period allows you to evaluate the relationship's long-term potential, ensuring it's a committed bond worth involving your children in.

Rushing into introductions can lead to confusion or jealousy for your children, especially if they perceive the new partner as threatening their relationship with you or your ex-spouse. When the time feels right, the setting of the introduction plays a pivotal role. Consider choosing neutral, casual environments, like a park or a favorite family restaurant, where your children feel relaxed and safe. These settings help ease the tension, providing a backdrop that encourages natural interactions.

Keep the initial meeting brief and informal, allowing everyone to get a feel for each other without the pressure of an extended, structured gathering. The goal is to create a positive first impression, laying the groundwork for future interactions. It's not about forcing a connection but allowing one to blossom organically, at its own pace.

Managing expectations is essential as you prepare for this introduction. Have an open discussion with your children beforehand, addressing their concerns. Explain that meeting your new partner doesn't change the love and attention they'll receive from you. Be honest about the new relationship, reinforcing that it doesn't alter their place in your life. Prepare your partner for the possibility of varied responses from your children. They might be curious, indifferent, or even resistant, and it's essential for your partner to understand that these reactions are normal. Please encourage them to be patient and respectful, allowing your children the space to adjust.

Open communication is the thread that weaves these elements together. Keeping the lines of dialogue open with your children about family changes fosters a sense of security and trust. Answer their questions honestly, providing reassurance while respecting their feelings. Please encourage them to share their thoughts and emotions about the new partner, whether excited, nervous, or unsure. This transparency helps them process their feelings and strengthens the bond between you and your children. By being upfront and supportive, you create an environment where they feel safe to express themselves, knowing their voices matter.

Interactive Element: Conversation Starters

Consider using conversation starters to facilitate discussions about the new partner with your children. Questions like "What do you hope to learn about [partner's name]?" or "How do you feel about meeting someone new?" can encourage them to open up and share their thoughts. This exercise can help reveal any underlying concerns or excitement, allowing you to address their feelings effectively.

Introducing a new partner to your children is a significant step in blending families, requiring sensitivity and careful planning. Choosing the right time, setting realistic expectations, and fostering open communication pave the way for smoother transitions and positive relationships. Remember, it's about creating a family dynamic where everyone feels valued and respected, allowing love to grow uniquely.

Author: Daniel McMahon

Fostering Positive Step-Sibling Relationships

Picture this: a living room filled with laughter as the kids work together to build a fort out of cushions and blankets. Moments of shared creativity begin to weave the threads of connection among step-siblings. Building these initial connections can sometimes feel like orchestrating a delicate dance, but it's worth every effort. Encouraging teamwork through joint activities helps break the ice. Whether it's a simple cooking project where everyone has a role or a DIY craft session, these shared tasks foster a sense of accomplishment and camaraderie. Family games, like board games or outdoor sports, serve as excellent icebreakers, prompting interaction in a fun, low-pressure setting. Outings, such as trips to the zoo or a nature hike, offer a change of scenery and an opportunity for everyone to explore and enjoy together, further strengthening these budding bonds.

But as with any family, conflicts will arise. When they do, having the tools to address these disputes constructively is crucial. One approach is mediation, where you step in as a neutral party to facilitate dialogue and help the children articulate their feelings and needs. Please encourage them to express their perspectives and listen to each other, fostering an environment where resolution, rather than blame, is the goal. Instituting household rules collaboratively can also help manage disputes. Sit together and discuss expectations and boundaries, allowing the children to have a say in their shared spaces' regulations. This democratic approach empowers them and instills a sense of responsibility and accountability.

Creating shared experiences is another vital piece of the puzzle. These are the memories that will stick, the ones that create a sense of family and belonging. Plan regular family outings or vacations that everyone can look forward to, whether a weekend camping trip or a day at an amusement park. These events are more than just fun; they're opportunities for bonding and creating a shared history. Involve the kids in family projects, like starting a garden or redecorating a room. These collaborative efforts can become cherished memories, with everyone contributing their unique touch to the outcome. Small rituals, like a weekly movie night or pizza-making session, can become traditions the kids anticipate and enjoy together.

While shared time is essential, balancing it with individual time and space is equally crucial. Each child needs the opportunity to pursue their interests and have a corner of the home that feels personal and private. Design a fair schedule for shared spaces like the living room or game room, ensuring everyone gets a turn and feels respected. Encourage each child to pursue hobbies that speak to them, whether playing an instrument, reading, or building model airplanes. This personal time allows them to recharge and develop a sense of individuality, essential for their growth and happiness. It also helps prevent feelings of competition or resentment, as each child recognizes their place and value within the family dynamic.

Author: Daniel McMahon

Visual Element: Activity Calendar

Create a family activity calendar and let each child contribute ideas for joint and individual activities. Use different colors to represent each child's input, ensuring everyone's voice is heard and valued. This visual tool helps keep track of plans and provides a fair balance between shared and individual time.

Fostering positive relationships among step-siblings aims to create an environment where each child feels seen, heard, and valued. It's about nurturing the unique dynamics of a blended family, where differences are celebrated, and new bonds are formed. You're laying the groundwork for a harmonious and supportive family environment through shared experiences, constructive conflict resolution, and balancing personal and family time.

Navigating Step-Parent Roles

Stepping into the role of a step-parent can sometimes feel like walking a tightrope. It's a delicate balance of asserting your presence while respecting the pre-existing dynamics within your new family. The first step in this balancing act is establishing clear roles and boundaries. This process begins long before any family meetings with the children. Having an open discussion with your partner, the biological parent, about what your role will look like is essential. What responsibilities will you take on, and where are the lines drawn?

These conversations can prevent misunderstandings and set expectations right from the start. It's a time to be candid about what each person needs to feel comfortable and respected in their roles. Once these discussions have taken place, it's essential to communicate these roles to the children clearly and age-appropriately. Explain what they can expect from you as a step-parent, reassuring them that you're there to support, not replace, their biological parents.

Building trust and respect is the foundation of any successful relationship, and step-parenting is no exception. One effective strategy is participating in activities that interest your stepchildren. Whether it's playing a game they love, watching their favorite movie, or attending their soccer matches, these shared experiences can create opportunities for bonding. It's not about forcing a connection but allowing one to develop naturally over time. Consistency is key in these interactions—show up regularly, keep your promises, and treat them fairly and respectfully. Children notice these efforts and, over time, trust and respect you in return. Remember, it's a marathon, not a sprint. Trust is earned slowly through actions and words that align over time.

Regarding discipline and authority, step-parents often find themselves in a tricky spot. Collaborating with the biological parent on discipline strategies ensures a united front. This might involve agreeing on rules and consequences that apply to all children in the household, stepchildren included. It's essential to have these discussions privately, away from the kids, to avoid undermining each other's authority. Once you agree on a strategy, present a united front when enforcing rules.

This consistency helps children understand the boundaries and expectations within the household. At the same time, step-parents should avoid taking on the primary disciplinarian role, especially in the early stages. Leaving discipline primarily to the biological parent can prevent resentment and help maintain a respectful relationship with the stepchildren.

Supporting the child's relationship with both biological parents is another critical aspect of the step-parent role. Encourage regular communication with both parents, fostering an environment where the child feels free to maintain these vital connections. It's not just about allowing phone calls or visits but actively supporting these interactions. Let's help them pick out a gift for their biological parent's birthday or remind them to call on special occasions. These actions show the child you respect and value their relationships, strengthening your bond. Avoid speaking negatively about the other parent, even if tensions exist. Children pick up on these cues, which can put them in an uncomfortable position. Instead, focus on positive reinforcement, highlighting the good moments and encouraging open dialogue about their feelings.

Navigating the role of a step-parent requires patience, empathy, and a lot of communication. It's about finding your place within the family structure and contributing to a harmonious environment where all members feel valued and respected. Each day presents opportunities to build stronger connections, foster trust, and create a loving home where everyone can thrive together.

Maintaining Traditions in Blended Families

The scent of cinnamon wafting through the house and the sound of laughter echoing off the walls are the building blocks of family traditions. Blending these cherished moments can be challenging and rewarding when two families come together. It's about taking the best from both worlds and creating something new that everyone can look forward to as a united family. Start with the holidays, those times of year steeped in rituals and customs. One family celebrates with a big Thanksgiving dinner, while the other always goes to a parade. Find ways to meld these traditions by having dinner and an evening outing. The key is to honor what each family holds dear while introducing new traditions that can be uniquely yours. Over time, these blended celebrations can become the heart of your family's story, weaving together past and present.

Respecting each family member's existing traditions is equally essential. Everyone comes with their customs, from the weekly Sunday roast to the annual summer camping trip. Allowing space for these traditions shows respect and understanding, acknowledging that each person's history is vital to who they are. Incorporate cultural or religious practices that hold meaning, whether lighting the menorah or setting up a nativity scene. These practices enrich the family experience and teach children the value of diversity and respect. By honoring these traditions, you create a tapestry of experiences that reflect the unique identities within the family, fostering a sense of belonging and continuity.

Celebrating diversity within your family is like opening a treasure chest full of rich stories and flavors. Imagine cooking meals from different family backgrounds, perhaps blending Grandma's Italian lasagna with Auntie's spicy curry. These culinary adventures can become family favorites, eagerly anticipated and joyfully shared. Learning about each other's family histories can be fascinating, providing context and understanding. You might discover shared values or see how similar traditions are expressed differently. These insights deepen family bonds and cultivate an appreciation for the rich tapestry of cultures and experiences that each member brings to the table.

Regular family meetings can be a cornerstone for planning these traditions and ensuring everyone has a say. Picture gathering around the kitchen table, a calendar in hand, as each member shares their ideas for upcoming events. These meetings can be a fun way to brainstorm, ensuring everyone's voice is heard and valued. Schedule seasonal planning sessions to map out the year's celebrations, from birthdays to holidays. Encourage input from all family members, even the youngest, as their perspectives can bring fresh ideas. This collaborative approach fosters a sense of inclusion. Planning is a shared responsibility, reinforcing that everyone is vital to the family unit.

As we wrap up this chapter, remember that traditions are not just about the past—they're living, breathing moments that connect us to our loved ones. By blending customs, respecting existing ones, and embracing diversity, you're crafting a family story that honors the past while building a future full of shared joy. In our next chapter, we'll explore the role of extended family involvement and enrich these new traditions.

CHAPTER 8

Extended Family Involvement

Imagine a bustling kitchen on a Sunday afternoon. The enticing aroma of freshly baked cookies fills the air. Laughter echoes off the walls as generations share stories and create memories. This is the heart of extended family involvement. This brings warmth and continuity to a child's life, especially after the upheaval of divorce. With their wealth of experience and unconditional love, Grandparents can play a pivotal role in this new family dynamic. They can be the anchor, providing stability and a sense of heritage that roots children in their family history, even as everything else seems to change.

Grandparents often step into co-parenting roles, intentionally or by necessity. They offer a unique perspective, acting as neutral confidants for the children.

Author: Daniel McMahon

In a world that might feel divided, grandparents can be the safe harbor where children share their thoughts without fear of judgment or conflict. This role of confidant is crucial, allowing children to process their emotions and fears in a supportive environment.

Grandparents, in their wisdom, can offer guidance not by telling children what to do but by sharing stories of their own experiences. These tales, often rich with lessons, help children navigate the complexities of their new reality.

Facilitating bonding activities can further strengthen the relationship between grandparents and grandchildren. Regular sleepovers or weekend visits can be an excellent way to spend time together, allowing children to enter a different world filled with bedtime stories and the comfort of a grandparent's embrace. These visits can be magical, offering a change of scenery and a break from the everyday hustle. Storytelling sessions about family history entertain and educate, creating a bridge between generations. Through these stories, children learn where they come from, reinforcing their identity and sense of belonging.

To ensure a cohesive family approach, it's vital to communicate parenting goals and values with grandparents. Aligning discipline and behavior expectations helps provide consistency, which is particularly important for unsettled children. Discuss educational goals and support needs openly. Grandparents can often offer invaluable support, whether helping with homework or attending school events. Their involvement in these areas shows children that their education is a shared priority, reinforcing its importance and providing additional motivation.

Grandparents can also seamlessly integrate into daily routines, enriching children's and parents' lives. Inviting them to school events or extracurricular activities allows them to share in the children's accomplishments and milestones. This involvement strengthens the bond with the grandchildren. It provides parents additional support and welcome relief in the busy world of co-parenting. Video calls for bedtime stories or regular check-ins can strengthen the connection, even if grandparents live far away. These virtual visits offer continuity and presence, a modern solution to bridge distances and maintain relationships.

Interactive Element: Grandparent-Grandchild Activity Planner

To help foster these connections, consider creating a shared activity planner. Please work with your children and their grandparents to list their favorite activities, from baking cookies to exploring local parks. Schedule regular times for these activities, ensuring that they become cherished rituals. This planner becomes a living document of shared experiences, a testament to the bonds being built.

In the tapestry of family life, grandparents add wisdom, stability, and love, weaving a more prosperous, supportive environment for children. Their involvement can be a powerful force, offering continuity and comfort as families navigate the challenges of co-parenting after divorce.

Author: Daniel McMahon

Balancing Extended Family Opinions

Navigating the varied opinions of extended family members can feel like herding cats, each with their distinct perspective shaped by unique life experiences. Recognizing and valuing these diverse viewpoints is crucial. Everyone, from your great-aunt with her old-school views to your sibling fresh out of college, brings something different. These differences can be rooted in generational gaps or cultural backgrounds, influencing how they perceive and interact with the family post-divorce. While Uncle Joe might think he knows best based on how things were done in the '60s, your teenage niece might have fresh insights that are more relevant today. It's important to listen respectfully, acknowledging that each perspective, though different, can contribute to a more affluent family dialogue. This doesn't mean you must agree with everyone, but understanding where they're coming from can foster empathy and reduce tension.

Setting boundaries for family involvement is like drawing a map with clear lines, showing everyone where they stand and what's expected of them. This is especially important when it comes to decision-making authority concerning your children. Let's face it: everyone has an opinion, but not everyone should have a say in every decision. Communicating clearly about who holds the reins in your child's life can prevent unnecessary interference. I suggest having a family meeting to outline these boundaries, making sure everyone knows who's responsible for what decisions.

This doesn't mean shutting down input but instead guiding it constructively. Guidelines on unsolicited advice are also essential—because while Grandma's advice on bedtime routines might be well-intentioned, it's okay to let her know that you've got it covered. It's all about balancing respect for their input with the autonomy you need as the primary caregiver.

Facilitating family meetings for input can be a game-changer in managing extended family dynamics. These gatherings, whether formal dinners or casual coffee sessions offer structured opportunities for everyone to share their thoughts constructively. Rotating the responsibility for hosting or leading these meetings can spread the burden, making everyone feel involved and valued. It's a bit like a potluck—everyone brings something to the table, adding to the shared experience. During these meetings, encourage family members to express their thoughts openly and remind them to listen actively. This can transform potential conflicts into collaborative problem-solving sessions where each voice is heard and respected.

Handling disagreements diplomatically is a skill that can save you a lot of headaches. When tensions rise, and they inevitably will, having strategies to manage conflicts can make a huge difference. Mediation techniques can effectively resolve disputes, offering a neutral space where each party can voice their concerns and work towards a solution. Encouraging active listening and empathy during these moments is key. It's about hearing what's said and understanding the emotions behind the words. This approach helps resolve the issue at hand. It strengthens family bonds, showing children how to manage conflicts with grace and understanding.

Visual Element: Family Meeting Agenda Template

To help facilitate these gatherings, consider creating a family meeting agenda template. Outline key topics to discuss, from decision-making processes to upcoming events, ensuring everyone has a chance to contribute. This agenda can serve as a guide, keeping discussions focused and productive while providing a record of what's been agreed upon for future reference.

Creating a Unified Support System

Building a strong support network is like constructing a safety net that holds everyone together. It's about identifying those key family members who can offer different types of support, creating a web of resources you can lean on. Imagine your cousin who teaches math stepping in to help with your child's homework, turning complex equations into fun learning experiences. Or your sister, a therapist, provides a listening ear and emotional guidance when things get tough. Recognize these strengths within your family and tap into them. Everyone might have something unique to offer, whether it's practical help or emotional support. By acknowledging these strengths, you create a culture of collaboration where everyone feels valued and appreciated.

Coordinating schedules for shared responsibilities might sound like a logistical nightmare, but it becomes much more manageable with open communication. Start by having candid conversations about availability and willingness to help. Your brother-in-law can take the kids to soccer practice on weekends, or your parents can handle school pickups on certain days. Use shared calendars to keep everyone in the loop, ensuring that tasks are evenly distributed and no one feels overwhelmed.

This coordination lightens your load and strengthens family bonds as everyone supports each other. It's about creating a rhythm where everyone plays their part, much like a symphony where each instrument contributes to the harmony.

Leveraging family strengths to address challenges is a game-changer in building a unified support system. Each family member brings unique skills and experiences that can be incredibly beneficial. For instance, that cousin who's a whiz at financial planning can help craft a budget that works for everyone involved. Or your aunt, who has a knack for organizing, can assist in planning family gatherings or celebrations. Recognizing these strengths empowers family members to contribute meaningfully, fostering a sense of purpose and belonging. It's about creating a team atmosphere where everyone feels valued and invested in the family's success.

Encourage collaborative problem-solving by fostering an environment where family challenges are approached as a team. Group brainstorming sessions can be a fun and productive way to tackle issues, whether planning a family vacation or deciding how to manage shared responsibilities. These sessions encourage creativity and open dialogue, allowing everyone to voice their ideas and concerns. It's not just about finding solutions; it's about building trust and understanding among family members. Family goal-setting activities can strengthen these bonds, as everyone works together towards common objectives. Whether saving for a big family trip or supporting a child's educational goals, setting and achieving goals as a family fosters unity and a sense of accomplishment.

Celebrating family milestones together is the glue that holds everything in place. Shared celebrations, like joint birthday parties or holiday gatherings, promote unity and create lasting memories.

These events are not just about the occasion itself but about the connections and traditions formed. Recognizing academic or personal accomplishments within the family is equally important. Whether it's a graduation, a new job, or an individual achievement, celebrating these milestones reinforces the support network and shows each family member they are valued and cherished. These celebrations are opportunities to express gratitude and love, strengthening the family's ties.

Textual Element: Family Strengths Worksheet

Consider creating a Family Strengths Worksheet to identify each member's unique skills and contributions. List everyone's strengths, from practical skills like cooking or gardening to emotional traits like empathy or resilience. Use this worksheet as a guide to delegate responsibilities and celebrate the diverse talents within your family. This exercise not only highlights each person's value but also fosters a deeper appreciation for the unique qualities that each family member brings to the table.

Encouraging Extended Family Communication

Picture this: a lazy Sunday afternoon where everyone from your family is scattered across the globe yet feeling connected. How? Through the wonders of modern communication. In a world where distances are bridged by technology, keeping open lines of communication with extended family becomes more vital than ever. It's not just about updating everyone on the latest family news—it's about fostering a sense of belonging and unity, no matter where each family member resides.

Family newsletters or group chats can be a fantastic way to keep everyone in the loop. Imagine sending out a monthly newsletter filled with not just updates but snippets of joy, such as a child's latest artwork or a new recipe tried by Aunt Susan. Group chats, whether on WhatsApp or another platform, allow daily interactions. These can be as simple as sharing a photo from a morning walk or as detailed as discussing plans for an upcoming family reunion. Scheduled phone calls or video conferences can take this one step further. They offer a chance to hear each other's voices and see familiar faces, making discussions more personal and connected. Whether it's a weekly check-in or a special occasion, these calls can become cherished traditions, bringing a little bit of home to wherever you are.

Promoting transparency and honesty within the family is crucial for maintaining trust and understanding. Encouraging honest feedback during family meetings helps ensure everyone's voice is heard and respected. It's about creating a safe space for family members to share their thoughts and feelings. Openness about family changes and decisions can prevent misunderstandings and build trust. Whether it's a new job, a move, or a change in family dynamics, being upfront with these changes keeps everyone informed and involved. It's about sharing the ups and downs, celebrating the good times, and supporting each other through the challenges.

Incorporating technology into family communications is a game-changer. Creating a family Facebook group or WhatsApp chat can provide a platform for sharing updates, photos, and videos. These digital spaces can be a treasure trove of memories, capturing everything from daily life to special events. Video call platforms for virtual gatherings can make family reunions possible, even when physical travel isn't. Picture a virtual dinner, where everyone from Grandma to the youngest cousin joins in from their dining tables, sharing a meal and stories as if they were all together in the same room. These tools are not just about convenience; they're about maintaining connections and nurturing relationships, ensuring no one feels left out or isolated.

Addressing communication barriers is key to ensuring everyone stays connected. Language differences or geographical distances can pose challenges but are not insurmountable. Consider using translation tools or services for family members who speak different languages. These can bridge communication gaps, ensuring everyone can participate fully in conversations. Generational gaps in technology use can also be a hurdle. Offering patience and guidance to those less tech-savvy can make a huge difference. Show Grandma how to use her tablet or help Uncle Joe set up his email. Simple gestures like these can empower family members who might otherwise feel excluded, bringing them into the fold and strengthening the family bond.

Maintaining open and effective communication with extended family is about more than just staying in touch; it's about creating a tapestry of connection that supports and uplifts everyone involved. Each interaction, whether big or small, adds a thread to this tapestry, weaving a network of love and support that spans generations and distances. As we embrace these strategies, we create inclusive, supportive, and resilient family dynamics, setting the stage for the next chapter of our journey together.

CHAPTER 9

Self-Care for Parents

Imagine standing in your kitchen, surrounded by the cheerful chaos of family life. The kids are laughing, the dog is barking, and dinner is bubbling away on the stove. Amid this whirlwind, losing sight of something significant, your well-being can be easy. As parents, our lives are often a balancing act, with self-care taking a backseat to the demands of everyday life. Yet, nurturing ourselves is not just a luxury—it's a necessity that enables us to be the best caregivers. This chapter is about prioritizing self-care, even on the busiest days.

Prioritizing Self-Care in a Busy Schedule

Self-care begins with identifying what truly nourishes you. It's about finding those activities that rejuvenate your spirit and give you the energy to tackle whatever life throws your way. For some, it might be a yoga class stretching the body and mind. For others, it could be as simple as a quiet moment with a good book. Start by creating a self-care checklist tailored to your interests and needs.

List activities that bring you joy and relaxation, whether gardening, painting, or taking a long bath. This list becomes your guide, reminding you of the importance of making time for yourself.

Incorporating these activities into your schedule requires intention. Allocate specific time slots for self-care as you would for any other necessary appointment. You may find a weekly yoga class that fits perfectly into your routine, or you may set aside time each evening for a calming ritual. These dedicated moments are essential for maintaining your well-being amidst the hustle and bustle of daily life. They serve as anchors, grounding you and providing stability and peace.

Micro-moments of self-care can also weave seamlessly into your day. Picture yourself savoring a cup of tea once the kids are off to school or pausing for a few deep breaths in the car before heading to work. These small, manageable moments of mindfulness can significantly impact your mental well-being. A morning meditation or a quick stretching routine can set a positive tone for the day. At the same time, a brief walk during lunch helps clear the mind and invigorate the body. Listening to your favorite music or a podcast while doing chores can transform mundane tasks into moments of joy and relaxation.

Time management tools are invaluable for carving out these self-care moments. A planner or scheduling app can help you block out time for self-care, ensuring it doesn't get lost in the shuffle of responsibilities. Consider creating a shared family calendar where everyone's activities are visible. This helps coordinate schedules and highlights dedicated self-care time, reinforcing its importance to you and your family. By making self-care a visible priority, you set a powerful example for your children, teaching them the value of balancing responsibilities with self-nurturing practices.

Another key aspect of prioritizing self-care is learning to say no. As parents, it's easy to feel obligated to meet every request, from volunteering at school to attending every social event. However, setting boundaries is crucial for preserving your energy and focus. Practice polite ways to decline invitations or requests that don't align with your priorities. It's okay to prioritize family and personal time over social obligations. Doing so creates space for the activities that truly matter, ensuring you have the energy and presence to engage fully with your loved ones.

Interactive Element: Self-Care Checklist

Use this checklist to identify and prioritize self-care activities:

1. List three activities that bring you joy.
2. Assign a specific time each week for one activity.
3. Identify one micro-moment of self-care you can practice daily.
4. Note one boundary you will set to protect your self-care time.

By embracing these strategies, you nurture your well-being and enhance your ability to care for those around you. Self-care is an ongoing journey that evolves with your needs and circumstances. It's about finding balance, honoring your needs, and creating a life that supports your health and happiness.

Stress Management Techniques for Parents

Stress has a sneaky way of creeping into our lives, especially when juggling parenting responsibilities. In those moments when you're trying to squeeze in a million tasks before bedtime, stress can feel overwhelming. But taking a step back to breathe can make all the difference. Mindfulness practices, like guided meditation, can help you find that much-needed pause. Apps like Headspace or Calm offer short sessions that fit easily into your day, providing moments of tranquillity amidst the chaos. These guided meditations can help center your thoughts, making tackling challenges with a calm mind easier. Another simple yet powerful technique is the 4-7-8 breathing exercise. You inhale for four counts, hold for seven, and exhale for eight. This rhythmic breathing slows your heart rate and promotes relaxation, making it a handy tool during stressful moments.

Physical activity is another fantastic way to combat stress. Exercise releases endorphins, those feel-good chemicals that boost your mood and help you tackle the day with a smile. Finding a local fitness class or joining a running group gets you moving and connects you with others who prioritize their well-being. If heading out isn't an option, home workout routines can be just as effective. Online videos offer everything from yoga to high-intensity interval training, allowing you to choose what fits your schedule and energy level. Even a brisk walk around the block can lift your spirits and clear your mind, making you feel more equipped to handle whatever comes your way.

Engaging in creative activities provides another outlet for stress relief. There's something incredibly soothing about expressing yourself through art. Painting, drawing, or crafting can become a meditative practice, allowing you to lose yourself and forget your worries for a while. Writing is another powerful tool. Whether journaling your thoughts or diving into creative writing exercises, putting pen to paper can help you process emotions and gain clarity. These creative outlets offer an escape and serve as a reminder of the joy that comes from doing something purely for pleasure.

Creating a stress-reducing environment at home can also significantly impact your mental well-being. Start by decluttering your space. A tidy environment reduces visual stressors and fosters a sense of calm. Imagine walking into a room where everything has its place and there's room to breathe. Soothing elements like soft lighting and calming scents can further enhance this tranquillity. Consider using lamps with warm bulbs and candles with scents like lavender or chamomile. These small changes can transform your home into a sanctuary where you can unwind and recharge.

Textual Element: Reflection Section

Reflect on your current stress management practices. Which mindfulness techniques or creative outlets resonate with you? Are there areas in your home that could be adjusted to create a more calming environment? Jot down a few ideas to explore and experiment with. By making these adjustments, you create space for relaxation and rejuvenation, helping you navigate the ups and downs of parenting with grace and resilience. This journey of self-discovery and care is ongoing, evolving as you do and offering new insights and practices to explore.

Overcoming Parental Guilt

Parenting often feels like a tightrope, balancing doing what's best for your kids and caring for yourself. And let's be honest, guilt is a constant companion for many parents. It sneaks up on you when you least expect it, whispering doubts about your time away from your children or how you handled last night's bedtime meltdown. Understanding where this guilt comes from is the first step in overcoming it. Maybe you feel guilty because work demands much of your time, leaving fewer hours to spend with your kids.

Or perhaps you're haunted by the idealized version of parenting that seems impossible to live up to. Recognizing these triggers allows you to step back and see them for what they are—natural feelings many parents experience, not reflections of your worth or abilities.

Once you've identified these sources of guilt, it's time to challenge the negative thoughts accompanying them. Cognitive techniques can be a game-changer here, helping you reframe those self-critical narratives that play on a loop in your mind. Gratitude is a powerful tool in this process. By shifting your focus to the joyous moments in your parenting journey, you can begin to appreciate the small victories instead of dwelling on perceived failures. Think about the laughter shared over a spilled bowl of cereal or the bedtime story that turned into an impromptu puppet show. These moments are reminders that you're doing your best, even when things don't go as planned. Affirmations are another effective strategy—positive statements reinforcing your self-worth and competence as a parent. Try starting your day with a simple mantra like, "I am enough, just as I am," echoing it when doubt creeps in.

Seeking validation from trusted sources is another way to combat parental guilt. Sometimes, the perspective of those who understand your situation can offer reassurance and support when you need it most. Conversations with a therapist or support group provide a safe space to express your feelings and gain insights from others in your shoes.

Friends and family members can offer valuable feedback, especially those who know your parenting style and values. Their encouragement can remind you of the love and dedication you pour into your family, even when you can't see it yourself. Surrounding yourself with supportive individuals creates a network of understanding that helps lighten the burden of guilt.

Embracing imperfection is a liberating step in overcoming parental guilt. It's about recognizing perfection as an unattainable standard that only adds unnecessary pressure. Parenting is messy, unpredictable, and beautifully imperfect, and that's okay. Delve into books or articles that embrace the concept of "good enough" parenting, focusing on love and connection rather than unattainable ideals. Engaging in self-compassion exercises can also be transformative. Allow yourself the grace to make mistakes and learn from them, just as you would encourage your child to do. Self-compassion involves treating yourself with kindness and understanding and acknowledging that everyone struggles, and that's part of being human. It might be as simple as taking a moment to breathe deeply and remind yourself that you're doing the best you can in this moment.

Textual Element: Reflection Section

Reflect on moments when you've felt parental guilt. Identify the triggers and consider how you can reframe these experiences with gratitude or affirmation. Note any supportive individuals in your life who can offer reassurance when needed. Explore resources on self-compassion and "good enough" parenting, and jot down your reflections and any insights gained. Embracing these practices can help you navigate the complexities of parenting with empathy and kindness, both for yourself and your children.

Author: Daniel McMahon

Building a Personal Support Network

A solid support network can be a lifeline in the whirlwind of daily life. It's like having a safety net beneath you, ready to catch you when things get tough. Start by identifying who in your circle can provide support. Friends and family members are often the first to come to mind. They know you well and can offer both emotional and practical help. Maybe it's your sister who's always there to lend an ear or a friend who can watch the kids for an afternoon. Recognizing these connections is the first step in leaning on them when needed.

Local parenting groups or online communities also offer a wealth of support. These spaces bring together individuals who understand the unique challenges of parenting. They provide a platform to share experiences, seek advice, and even find encouragement. Joining a local group can lead to friendships that provide both laughter and solace. Online communities, on the other hand, offer the flexibility to engage on your schedule. Perhaps there's a group focused on single parents, or you connect with others who share your child's interests. These connections can benefit your support network, offering diverse perspectives and understanding.

Cultivating meaningful relationships requires intention and effort. It's about nurturing existing bonds and creating new ones. Consider scheduling regular catch-ups with friends or family. It could be as simple as a monthly coffee date or a walk in the park. These moments of connection remind us of the strength and joy found in relationships.

Joining clubs or groups that align with personal interests is another way to meet like-minded individuals. Whether it's a book club or a hiking group, these activities provide opportunities to connect with others who share your passions, strengthening your support network.

There are times when professional support can be incredibly beneficial. Whether you're navigating the complexities of co-parenting or seeking personal growth, professionals offer guidance and insight. Engaging with a life coach or counselor can provide a safe space to explore challenges and work towards solutions. These professionals bring expertise and an outside perspective that can be invaluable. Workshops or seminars on personal development also offer opportunities to learn and grow. They provide tools and techniques to enhance your well-being and enrich your life.

Building a support network isn't just about receiving help; it's also about giving. Fostering reciprocal support strengthens relationships and builds community. Consider organizing a babysitting swap with other parents. It's a simple way to lighten the load and offer each other a break. Hosting regular gatherings where friends can share experiences is another way to foster connection. It could be a potluck dinner or a weekend BBQ. These gatherings create a space for sharing stories, laughter, and support. They remind us that we're all in this together, navigating the ups and downs of life with the help of those we care about.

In the end, building a personal support network is about connection. It's about surrounding yourself with people who uplift and inspire you while also being there to offer support in return. These relationships become a source of strength, providing comfort and encouragement when needed. They remind us that we're not alone and can face whatever challenges come our way together.

As we wrap up this chapter, it's clear that prioritizing self-care and building a support network is key to navigating the complexities of parenting. These elements empower us to be present and engaged for ourselves and our families. Next, we'll explore practical tools and strategies to enhance our co-parenting experience, providing clarity and direction as we move forward.

CHAPTER 10

Practical Tools and Strategies

Have you ever found yourself in the middle of a family gathering, surrounded by laughter and loved ones, only to feel uncertain about how the future will unfold for your children after a divorce? You're not alone. Parents in similar situations worry about providing stability and structure in an upside-down world. This chapter aims to turn that uncertainty into confidence by giving a practical blueprint for co-parenting that caters to the complex needs of a family split across two households. Let's explore how crafting a comprehensive parenting plan can offer clarity and peace of mind.

Creating a parenting plan is akin to assembling a puzzle. Each piece fits together to create a picture of your child's future. This plan should include essential components, each carefully thought out to ensure nothing is left to chance. Start with custody and visitation schedules, the backbone of any parenting plan. Considering school activities, holidays, and weekends, these schedules must reflect your availability and your child's needs. Clearly defined time slots can prevent misunderstandings and ensure both parents have ample opportunity to engage in their child's life.

Equally important are communication protocols between parents. Determine how you will communicate—whether through co-parenting apps, email, or face-to-face meetings—and set boundaries to ensure that discussions remain respectful and focused on your child's well-being. Furthermore, it outlines decision-making responsibilities for major child-related issues like education, healthcare, and extracurricular activities. Decide who will make these decisions or if they will be shared to prevent conflicts.

Flexibility is the lifeline of a successful parenting plan. Life is unpredictable, and a rigid plan can quickly become obsolete when unforeseen circumstances arise. It's crucial to incorporate procedures for handling schedule changes—perhaps allowing for a certain number of swaps per year or agreeing to review the schedule quarterly. Contingency plans are equally important for emergencies, providing a clear path for both parents to follow when the unexpected happens.

This could involve designating a trusted third party if neither parent is available or establishing protocols for medical emergencies. Flexibility isn't about giving up control; it's about ensuring that your plan can adapt to the ebbs and flows of life, providing a safety net for your child's well-being.

Financial responsibilities should be meticulously detailed in the parenting plan. To avoid ambiguity, include child support payment schedules, specifying due dates and payment methods. Additionally, it addresses shared expenses for extracurricular activities and healthcare, clarifying how costs will be divided and reimbursed. This transparency fosters trust between co-parents and ensures that financial obligations are met consistently, supporting your child's development and well-being. Consider using apps like OurFamilyWizard, which can document child support payments and shared expenses, providing a clear record for both parties and reducing potential disputes.

Drafting a parenting plan with legal guidance is wise to ensure its comprehensiveness and enforceability. Consulting with a family law attorney can provide valuable insights into state-specific legal requirements, helping you create a plan that stands up in court if necessary. A lawyer can review the plan, highlighting potential issues you might have overlooked and ensuring that your rights—and your child's best interests—are protected. Legal advice isn't just about compliance; it's about crafting a fair, realistic plan tailored to your family's unique needs.

Interactive Element: Parenting Plan Template

Consider using a parenting plan template to organize your thoughts and ensure no detail is overlooked. This template can guide you through each section, from visitation schedules to decision-making responsibilities, offering prompts to help you articulate your preferences and priorities. Having a structured format can make a daunting task more manageable, providing clarity and direction as you navigate the complexities of co-parenting.

Crafting a comprehensive parenting plan is more than logistics; it's about creating a stable, nurturing environment for your child to thrive in. By carefully considering each component and allowing room for flexibility, you can build a plan that supports your child's growth and happiness, providing peace of mind for you and your co-parent.

Author: Daniel McMahon

Utilizing Checklists and Calendars for Organization

Imagine waking up to a busy school day, rushing your kids through breakfast, only to realize you've forgotten something essential at home. It could be the lunchbox sitting on the kitchen counter or the library book due last week. We've all been there. That's where custom checklists come in handy. They act like a friendly reminder for all those little tasks that slip through the cracks. Start with a morning routine checklist for school days.

List everything from brushing teeth and packing lunch to grabbing the right backpack. It helps streamline those hectic mornings and ensures nothing important is left behind. Having a packing list is a lifesaver regarding shared custody transitions. A checklist provides a smoother transition between homes, whether it's ensuring your child has their favorite toy or all their school supplies.

Digital calendars are another fantastic tool for managing the myriad of events and responsibilities that fill our lives. With apps like Google Calendar, you can easily sync family events, allowing everyone to stay on the same page. It's not just about school schedules or extracurricular activities—it's about creating a seamless flow of information that keeps the whole family connected. Setting up reminders for necessary appointments or deadlines can prevent those last-minute scrambles. Imagine getting a gentle nudge on your phone about the parent-teacher meeting or the dentist appointment you scheduled months ago. These digital nudges help you manage your time better, reducing stress and ensuring you're always prepared.

Recurring events are a staple in family life, and planning for them can turn chaos into cherished traditions. For instance, weekly family dinners or game nights offer a consistent opportunity for connection and conversation, fostering a sense of stability and belonging. Monthly check-ins with teachers or coaches can inform you about your child's progress and any areas needing attention. By scheduling these regular commitments, you prioritize family time and create a rhythm everyone can count on. It's about making time for what matters most and ensuring that these moments of connection are protected.

Coordinating with your co-parent using organizational tools can transform your co-parenting relationship. Sharing calendar access with your co-parent lets you see the complete picture of your child's schedule, minimizing misunderstandings and fostering cooperation. Weekly scheduling meetings can further enhance this collaboration. Set aside weekly time to align plans, discuss upcoming changes, and address concerns. This proactive approach not only improves communication but also builds trust and partnership. When both parents work together, it creates a more supportive environment for your child, allowing them to thrive without feeling caught in the middle.

Visual Element: Custom Checklist Template

Crafting a custom checklist can be as simple as jotting down tasks on paper or using a digital template. Begin by listing daily tasks for school days or custody transitions. As you go through your day, check off each task, allowing for the satisfaction of crossing things off a list. This simple tool offers peace of mind, ensuring nothing crucial is overlooked, and brings a sense of accomplishment with every completed task.

Author: Daniel McMahon

Implementing Effective Routine Changes

Picture this: It's a typical weekday morning, and the house is buzzing with activity. Cereal bowls clink, kids scramble to find that missing shoe, and the clock ticks ever closer to when you need to leave. Amidst this whirlwind, you might wonder if there's a more efficient way to get everyone out the door with less stress. This is where assessing your current routines becomes crucial. Take a step back and observe your daily patterns. Are there moments where everything seems to bottleneck, causing unnecessary tension? The kids may be all vying for the bathroom simultaneously, or maybe breakfast prep is more chaotic than it needs to be. Identifying these stress points can reveal inefficiencies, offering a clear direction for improvement. Look at how time is managed throughout the day. Are there periods where things feel rushed or disorganized? Pinpointing these areas opens the door to smoother mornings and less hectic evenings.

Once you have a clear picture of what's not working, the next step is introducing changes—but slowly. The key is making minor, incremental adjustments rather than overhauling everything. This could mean staggering bathroom times or prepping breakfast items the night before. Minor tweaks can lead to significant improvements without overwhelming your family. Remember, it's all about minimizing disruption and resistance. Change can be difficult, especially for kids who thrive on routine. Allow time for everyone to adapt to new schedules. Start with minor alterations and gradually build upon them, giving each change a chance to settle before adding more. These gradual shifts can help everyone adjust comfortably, leading to a more harmonious household.

Involving your children in planning these new routines can make a difference. When kids feel they have a say in their daily schedule, they're more inclined to cooperate. Hold family meetings to discuss potential changes. Let everyone voice their thoughts and ideas. You might be surprised by the practical suggestions your kids provide. They may come up with a creative way to streamline the morning rush, or they may suggest a new evening wind-down activity. Encouraging them to propose their ideas increases buy-in and empowers them, fostering a sense of responsibility and teamwork. It transforms the process from a top-down directive to a collaborative effort where everyone feels valued and heard.

Monitoring and adjusting routines as needed is another crucial element. Life is dynamic, and what works today might not work tomorrow. Regularly review your routines to ensure they remain practical and relevant. Consider setting aside time for monthly reflection sessions. These can be informal gatherings where you assess what's working, what isn't, and what might need tweaking. Be open to feedback and willing to make adjustments. This flexibility is vital in adapting to your family's evolving needs. Whether accommodating a new after-school activity or adjusting to seasonal changes, being willing to pivot can help maintain balance and harmony in your household. Remember, routines are not set in stone—they're living, breathing frameworks that should grow alongside your family.

Textual Element: Routine Reflection Journal

Consider keeping a Routine Reflection Journal. Use it to jot down notes about your family's daily flow, highlighting areas of success and those needing improvement. Encourage each family member to contribute their thoughts. Over time, this journal can become a valuable resource, offering insights into how your routines evolve and adapt to meet your family's needs. It's a living document that captures the ebb and flow of your household, providing a foundation for continued growth and improvement.

Leveraging Community Resources

You might find yourself staring at the ceiling late at night, pondering how to juggle co-parenting responsibilities. It's a familiar feeling that can be alleviated by tapping into the available community resources. Community centers, often the heart of local life, offer a variety of parenting workshops that can provide valuable insights and skills. These workshops are more than just educational sessions; they're a chance to connect with others who understand your unique challenges. Libraries, too, can be a treasure trove of support. Many offer free family activities and events designed to foster connection and learning. Whether it's a reading circle or a craft day, these events provide a space for you and your children to relax and engage with your community.

Engaging with support networks can be incredibly empowering. Parenting groups or clubs, especially those tailored for single parents, offer a safe space to share experiences and gather advice. These groups can be a lifeline, providing practical tips and emotional support from people who genuinely get what you're going through.

Online forums are another excellent resource, allowing you to connect with local parents from home. These digital communities offer a platform for asking questions, sharing stories, and building friendships that can transcend the internet. It's reassuring to know that, even when you feel isolated, others are walking a similar path, ready to offer support and understanding.

Education is another avenue worth exploring, both for yourself and your children. Childcare and early education programs can give your little ones a strong foundation, setting them up for success. Meanwhile, adult education or skills workshops can help you enhance your parenting skills or pursue new career opportunities. Many community centers offer classes on everything from cooking and budgeting to resume writing and interview skills. These programs equip you with practical knowledge and boost your confidence, reminding you that growth and learning don't stop just because you're a parent.

Health and wellness resources are equally important in ensuring family well-being. Many communities offer free or low-cost health clinics that provide essential medical services without straining your budget. These clinics can be a lifesaver, providing everything from routine check-ups to vaccinations. Mental health support services are another invaluable resource. Whether seeking counsel for yourself or support for your child, these services can help you navigate the emotional complexities of post-divorce life. Therapists and counselors offer a safe space to explore feelings and work through challenges, providing tools and strategies to foster resilience and healing.

Author: Daniel McMahon

Resource List: Community Support Services

Compile a list of local community resources, including addresses, contact information, and a brief description of their services. Consider including community centers, libraries, parenting workshops, support groups, and health clinics. Having this information at your fingertips can be incredibly helpful when you need support or guidance.

By leveraging these community resources, you're not just getting support for yourself; you're building a network that benefits your entire family. Access to these services enriches your life and provides opportunities to grow, learn, and connect with others. Each resource you tap into contributes to a stronger, more resilient family unit capable of weathering the changes that divorce brings. As we move forward, remember that while the challenges of co-parenting can seem daunting, the support of your community can make all the difference. In the next chapter, we'll explore future-focused parenting incorporating technologies, you're enhancing their learning and nurturing a lifelong love for discovery.

CHAPTER 11

Future-Focused Parenting

Picture this: your child, nestled comfortably on the couch, tablet in hand, eyes wide with curiosity as they navigate an educational app that's teaching them complex math concepts with the ease of a game. This scene is a far cry from the chalkboards and textbooks many of us grew up with, yet it's the reality of parenting in the digital age. Two-thirds of U.S. parents feel that parenting is more challenging now than two decades ago, mainly due to the pervasive presence of technology. While it offers unprecedented opportunities for learning and connectivity, it also presents challenges that demand a delicate balance between embracing the benefits and mitigating the risks. This chapter will equip you with the tools to leverage technology to enhance your child's development while safeguarding their well-being.

Author: Daniel McMahon

Embracing Technological Advances in Parenting

Educational technology is a beacon of possibility in this rapidly evolving digital landscape. Platforms like Khan Academy have revolutionized how children learn, offering interactive lessons catering to various learning styles. Whether mastering algebra or exploring the intricacies of biology, these resources provide a personalized learning experience that can complement traditional education. Imagine your child delving into a history lesson where they can watch animated timelines unfold, making the past come alive in vibrant detail. Interactive storytelling tools further enrich this experience, drawing children into narratives that entertain and build critical literacy skills. By incorporating these technologies, you're enhancing their learning and nurturing a lifelong love for discovery.

However, with these opportunities come responsibilities. As parents, guiding our children to navigate digital spaces safely and responsibly is paramount. With 71% of parents expressing concern over the potential harm smartphones can cause young children, understanding and managing these risks is crucial. Start by familiarizing yourself and your child with privacy settings on social media platforms. These settings act as a protective barrier, controlling who can view and interact with your child's content. Educate them on recognizing and reporting online bullying or unsafe content, empowering them to take control of their digital interactions. By instilling these skills, you're protecting them and fostering digital literacy that will serve them well into adulthood.

Balancing screen time with other activities is another essential aspect of healthy tech use. Establishing family tech-free zones or hours can help create a routine where devices are put aside for face-to-face interactions. This might mean having a tech-free dinner table, where conversations flow freely without the distraction of screens. Please encourage your children to engage in outdoor play and physical activities, which benefit their physical health and enhance their social skills and creativity. By setting these boundaries, you're teaching them the importance of moderation and helping them develop a balanced lifestyle.

Technology also offers unique ways to strengthen family bonds, especially when distance is a factor. Video calls with distant relatives can bridge the physical gap, allowing your child to maintain meaningful relationships with family members who live far away. Imagine the joy on your child's face as they share stories and laughter with grandparents over a video call, feeling connected despite the miles between them. Consider creating a shared family blog or photo album where everyone can contribute and stay updated on each other's lives. These digital tools keep families close and create a shared history that can be cherished for years.

Interactive Element: Family Digital Literacy Contract

Consider developing a Family Digital Literacy Contract. This can be a fun, collaborative activity where you and your child list rules and agreements for tech use. Discuss privacy settings, online etiquette, and the importance of balance. Make it a living document, revisiting and updating it as your child grows and technology evolves. This contract sets clear expectations and empowers your child to take responsibility for their digital presence.

In this age of screens, it's easy to feel overwhelmed by the pace of technological change. But by embracing these advances thoughtfully, you can transform the digital landscape from a source of anxiety into a platform for growth and connection.

Preparing Children for Social Changes

Imagine your child in a classroom, surrounded by peers from all walks of life, each bringing unique stories and backgrounds. It's a rich tapestry that reflects the world we live in. Teaching kids to embrace diversity and inclusion becomes beneficial and necessary in this setting. Start by introducing them to books and media celebrating different cultures and perspectives. Whether through a vivid tale of an African safari or a documentary about life in a bustling Asian metropolis, these stories can open their minds to the vastness of human experience. Encouraging participation in multicultural community events further deepens this understanding. For example, attending a local festival that celebrates a culture different from your own can be an eye-opening experience for a child. It's an opportunity to taste new foods, hear new music, and see the beauty in diversity. These experiences plant seeds of curiosity and respect, which can flourish into a lifelong appreciation for the differences that make our world so vibrant.

As our children grow, they inevitably encounter social issues requiring thoughtful discussion. Topics like environmental awareness and sustainability have become central to modern life, and children are often eager to learn how they can make a difference. Simple practices, like recycling or conserving water, can become powerful lessons in responsibility and stewardship. These are not just chores but acts of caring for the planet. Conversations about equality and respect for all individuals are equally crucial. Discussing the importance of treating everyone with kindness, regardless of race, gender, or background, helps instill values of fairness and empathy. Use age-appropriate language to ensure they understand the significance of these issues and feel empowered to contribute positively.

Empathy and compassion are cornerstones of a well-rounded individual, and teaching these qualities can start early. Volunteering within the community offers a hands-on way for children to practice empathy. Whether it's helping out at a local food bank or participating in a neighborhood cleanup, these activities teach them to look beyond themselves and consider the needs of others. Role-playing scenarios can also be an effective tool. Children can develop a deeper understanding of different perspectives by acting out situations where they must put themselves in someone else's shoes. This practice nurtures their ability to relate to others, fostering a compassionate outlook that will serve them well throughout life.

Children today face a rapidly changing world, and adaptability is key to thriving in such an environment. Preparing them to handle social changes and transitions with resilience is one of the greatest gifts we can give them. Please encourage them to make new friends in different settings, whether at school, in sports, or through community activities. This broadens their social circle and teaches them to be open-minded and accepting. Supporting their openness to new experiences and ideas helps them become flexible thinkers, ready to embrace whatever comes their way. Please encourage them to try new activities, explore different interests, and be willing to step out of their comfort zones. These experiences build confidence and adaptability, equipping them to face the unknown with courage.

In this ever-evolving social landscape, guiding your child through these changes requires patience, understanding, and a willingness to learn alongside them. By fostering an environment where diversity is celebrated, social issues are discussed openly, and empathy is practiced daily, you're laying a strong foundation for their future interactions. These lessons go beyond the classroom, shaping them into individuals aware of and eager to contribute positively to the world around them. As they navigate this complex world, they do so with the knowledge that they are supported, valued, and capable of making a difference.

Adapting to New Family Structures

Imagine waking up to a household that feels different every day. This is often the reality in families adjusting to new dynamics. Whether it's a new job that pulls one parent away from the home more often or the addition of a step-sibling, these shifts can change the landscape of family life. Understanding these evolving roles is crucial. You may have taken on more cooking duties while balancing work-from-home tasks, or perhaps the kids are now helping out more with household chores. As responsibilities shift, it's essential to communicate openly about these changes. Acknowledging how roles evolve helps everyone feel valued and heard. It's about recognizing that family isn't static; it's a living, breathing entity that grows and changes over time.

Open, honest discussions become the glue that holds everyone together when families change. Regular family meetings can be an excellent tool for addressing new living arrangements or shifts in daily routines. These meetings don't have to be formal; consider them a safe space where everyone can share their thoughts and feelings. It's a chance to sit down and talk about how everyone's adapting and what might need tweaking. Encourage each family member to voice their feelings about the changes, creating a dialogue that fosters understanding and empathy. By having these open conversations, you teach your children that expressing their emotions is okay and that their opinions matter. This practice helps manage current changes and equips them with the skills to handle future transitions gracefully and confidently.

Maintaining family cohesion amidst change requires intentional effort. Scheduling regular family check-ins or bonding activities can help strengthen connections. These could be as simple as a weekly game night or a monthly outing to a favorite park. The key is consistency, creating a rhythm that the family can rely on. Another powerful tool is crafting a family mission statement or vision. This isn't just a motivational exercise; it's about clarifying what values and goals your family holds dear. It could be a commitment to kindness, adventure, or learning. Whatever it is, this shared vision can act as a guiding light, especially during times of change. It reminds everyone of the bigger picture and the shared goals that bind you together.

In today's world, families come in all shapes and sizes, each beautiful. Celebrating diverse family models isn't just about accepting differences but embracing and cherishing them. One way to do this is by exploring stories and media representing various family types. Books and movies that showcase different family structures can be eye-opening and affirming for children. They offer a window into other worlds and validate the uniqueness of your own family. Participating in family diversity events or workshops can also be a fun and enriching experience. These gatherings allow one to meet others who share similar experiences, fostering a sense of community and belonging.

It's important to remember that adapting to new family structures is a process, not a one-time event. It requires patience, understanding, and a willingness to adapt. As each family member finds their footing in this new dynamic, there will be moments of learning and growth. Embracing these changes with an open heart and mind can lead to deeper connections and a stronger family bond.

Remember that every family is unique, and there is no one-size-fits-all approach. What matters most is creating an environment where everyone feels loved, supported, and valued. This is the foundation upon which a happy, thriving family is built.

Fostering Independence and Responsibility

Imagine your child, sleeves rolled up, diligently watering the plants, or feeding the family pet. It's a simple task but a decisive step towards fostering responsibility and independence. Assigning age-appropriate chores is more than just a way to lighten the load at home; it's an opportunity for your child to take on responsibilities that match their developmental stage. Younger children might enjoy helping with tasks like sorting laundry or setting the table. At the same time, older kids could manage more complex duties such as cooking a simple meal or taking the dog for a walk.

Chore charts can be a fun and effective way to keep track of these tasks. They offer a visual reminder of what needs to be done and provide a sense of accomplishment when a job is completed. As your child checks off each task, they gain confidence and learn the value of contributing to the family unit.

Encouraging decision-making skills is another key aspect of nurturing independence. It's about giving children the tools to make informed choices and understand the consequences of those choices. Start by involving them in planning family activities, like choosing a weekend outing or deciding what to have for dinner. These decisions may seem small, but they teach valuable lessons in weighing options and considering outcomes. When children see the impact of their choices—whether it's the joy of a family day at the park or the satisfaction of a well-prepared meal—they learn to appreciate the responsibility of making decisions. Discussing the potential consequences of their choices helps them understand the importance of thinking ahead. It's a skill that will serve them well in all areas of life, from friendships to academics to future careers.

Setting and achieving personal goals is a powerful way to foster a sense of accomplishment and self-worth. Please encourage your child to set academic or individual targets, whether improving a math grade or mastering a new skill like playing an instrument. Help them break these goals into manageable steps and celebrate each milestone. Recognition of their efforts—whether through verbal praise, a small reward, or a special outing—reinforces their motivation and commitment. Participation in extracurricular activities is another excellent avenue for goal-setting. Whether joining a sports team, participating in a school club, or engaging in volunteer work, these activities build skills, foster teamwork, and provide a sense of belonging. They also offer a platform for children to set personal goals and experience the satisfaction of achieving them.

Author: Daniel McMahon

Balancing guidance with freedom is the most delicate part of fostering independence. As parents, it's natural to want to protect our children from mistakes. Still, allowing them room to explore and learn from their experiences is essential. Setting safe boundaries provides a framework within which they can safely navigate their world. These boundaries include curfews, screen time limits, or social interaction guidelines. Please encourage your child to explore their interests and take on challenges within these limits. Offer support and advice when needed, but resist the urge to micromanage.

Trust in their decision-making ability, and be there to guide them if they stumble. This balance of freedom and support helps build resilience, teaching children that mistakes are a part of life and opportunities for growth. As you encourage your child's journey towards independence, remember that each step is a step towards becoming a confident, capable individual. By nurturing responsibility, decision-making, and goal-setting skills, you equip them with the tools they need to navigate life's challenges with courage and confidence.

Chapter 12

Encouragement and Reflection

Standing in the remnants of what once was a shared life, you might wonder how to piece together a new one. With its tangled web of emotions and logistics, divorce often leaves you feeling like a jigsaw puzzle with missing pieces. Yet, within this upheaval exists a powerful opportunity for personal growth. This chapter invites you to pause and reflect on your journey through divorce and co-parenting, encouraging you to celebrate your progress and identify areas where further growth awaits. Let's explore how your experiences have shaped you and how you can continue to evolve into the best version of yourself for you and your children.

Reflecting on personal growth begins with a simple question: how have you changed since the divorce? Journaling can be a powerful tool, offering a safe space to explore your transformation. Consider prompts like "What strengths have I discovered in myself?" or "Which moments challenged me the most, and how did I handle them?"

These reflections can reveal a deeper understanding of your resilience and coping strategies. Perhaps you've learned to communicate more effectively or set boundaries honoring your needs. Embrace these discoveries as milestones on your path to personal empowerment. Recognizing the growth in yourself not only boosts your confidence but also sets a positive example for your children.

The challenges you've faced often carry valuable lessons. Reflecting on these insights can illuminate new family dynamics and conflict resolution perspectives. You may have developed the ability to de-escalate heated situations or learned to listen more empathetically. Understanding these lessons allows you to approach future challenges with a toolbox of strategies. It also helps you see past adversities not as setbacks but as stepping stones to a more harmonious family life. Acknowledge the wisdom you've gained, and consider how these insights can guide you in fostering a nurturing environment for your children.

However, growth doesn't mean you've reached the finish line. It's important to recognize areas where you still encounter difficulties. Communication issues occasionally arise when coordinating schedules or discussing sensitive topics with your co-parent. Identifying these patterns is the first step in addressing them. Similarly, maintaining self-care routines might be a struggle amidst the demands of parenting and work. Acknowledge these ongoing challenges without judgment, viewing them as opportunities for continued growth. By accepting where you are, you can chart a course for where you want to be.

Creating a personal growth plan can provide direction and motivation. Start by setting actionable goals for further emotional healing. You may aim to attend a workshop on conflict resolution or explore courses that enhance your parenting skills. These steps contribute to your personal development and enrich your family life. Consider incorporating practices like mindfulness or gratitude into your daily routine, fostering a mindset of positivity and resilience. Your growth plan is a roadmap, guiding you toward a more fulfilling and balanced life.

Interactive Element: Journaling Prompts

Reflect on these questions in your journal: "What have I learned about myself since the divorce?" "How have I grown as a parent?" "What ongoing challenges do I face?" "What steps can I take to continue my personal development?" Use these reflections to create your growth plan, detailing specific actions in the coming months.

As you continue your journey, remember that growth is not a destination but a lifelong process. Each step forward, no matter how small, brings you closer to the life you envision for yourself and your family. Embrace this opportunity with courage and curiosity, knowing that every challenge holds the potential for transformation.

Setting Long-Term Family Goals

Imagine a moment of stillness where you close your eyes and picture what you genuinely want for your family. Think about the laughter echoing through your home, the milestones celebrated, and the quiet evenings spent together. This is where it begins—the envisioning stage. It's about dreaming big and considering what kind of future you want to create.

Author: Daniel McMahon

Perhaps it's a vision filled with family traditions passed down through generations or a home where new traditions are born. Visualization exercises can help bring these dreams into focus, allowing you to explore what family values are most important. Maybe it's kindness, resilience, or open communication. When you take the time to visualize, you plant the seeds for what will eventually grow into your family's future.

Once you have a clear picture, it's time to define specific goals that align with this vision. These aren't just dreams—they're actionable steps that bring you closer to your desired family life. Start with educational goals for your children. Consider what success looks like for them, whether it's academic achievements, pursuing passions, or simply being happy and curious learners. Discuss these aspirations together, allowing your children to express their dreams and ambitions. Then, think about long-term financial plans. Creating a stable foundation is crucial for peace of mind and enabling opportunities like family vacations, educational pursuits, and future security. Setting these goals requires collaboration and open dialogue, ensuring everyone understands and supports the path forward.

Aligning individual and family objectives is vital in nurturing a harmonious household. While each family member has personal goals and ambitions, ensuring they contribute to the family's overall well-being is essential. Balancing career aspirations with family time can be challenging, yet it's necessary for maintaining strong connections. You may aspire to advance in your career but also want to be present at your child's soccer games or school performances.

Finding this balance might mean setting boundaries at work or scheduling regular family activities. Encourage your children to set personal goals that align with family harmony. Whether helping with chores, excelling in school, or simply showing kindness, these goals can reinforce the values you cherish as a family.

Monitoring progress and adjusting goals as needed is key to staying on track. Life is unpredictable, and circumstances change, so flexibility is essential. Hold regular family meetings to check how everyone is doing with their goals. Celebrate successes and address any challenges, maintaining an open and supportive atmosphere. If a goal is no longer relevant or achievable, adapt it to suit your current situation better. This approach keeps everyone accountable and reinforces that goals are a dynamic part of life, evolving as you do.

Interactive Element: Family Vision Board

Gather as a family to create a vision board. Use magazines, pictures, and art supplies to represent your dreams and goals. Display it in a common area as a reminder of your shared aspirations and the journey you're embarking on together.

Remember, setting long-term family goals is not just about reaching a destination. It's about the journey you take together, the lessons you learn, and the bonds you strengthen in pursuing a shared vision. As you move forward, embrace each new day's possibilities and continue to support one another with love, understanding, and encouragement.

Celebrating Milestones and Successes

In the hustle and bustle of daily life, it's easy to overlook the small victories that mark our progress. Yet, these moments deserve recognition just as much as the significant milestones. From the first morning, you manage to get everyone out the door on time, and the first evening, your child opens up about their day without prompting. These are the moments that illuminate our path. Creating a family achievement board or scrapbook can be an excellent way to capture these successes. It becomes a visual reminder of how far you've come—a place where each family member can contribute, adding their achievements and celebrating others'. This practice fosters community and shared pride, transforming everyday achievements into cherished memories.

Celebrations don't have to be grand to be meaningful. Sometimes, it's the simple acts that resonate the most. Consider planning special family outings to mark achievements, like a picnic at a favorite park or a night out for ice cream. These outings serve as both a reward and a bonding experience, reinforcing the idea that success is a family affair. You might even craft personalized awards or certificates to honor specific achievements, whether for mastering a new skill, improving communication, or simply being kind. These tangible tokens of recognition can be powerful motivators, reminding each family member of their unique contributions and growth.

Reflecting on your collective journey can be as enriching as the celebrations themselves. Consider creating a timeline of key family events, a tangible representation of the path you've walked together. This timeline can include everything from significant milestones to the quieter, intimate moments that have shaped your family's narrative. Sharing stories of growth and change during family gatherings can spark conversations filled with laughter and nostalgia, reinforcing the bonds that tie you together. It's about acknowledging where you started and appreciating the resilience and determination that have brought you to where you are now.

Incorporating gratitude practices into your daily routine can amplify the joy of celebrating successes. A family gratitude journal is a simple yet profound tool for recording positive moments. Each evening, take a few minutes to jot down something you're grateful for. It could be as significant as a promotion at work or as simple as a delicious dinner shared. These entries remind you of the abundance in your lives, shifting focus from what's lacking to what's already present. Sharing daily gratitude at family meals can also foster a spirit of appreciation and connection. As each person shares what they're thankful for, you create a tapestry of gratitude that underscores the richness of your shared experiences.

Visual Element: Family Gratitude Journal

Transform an ordinary notebook into a family gratitude journal. Dedicate a few minutes each evening for family members to write down one thing they're grateful for. Over time, this journal becomes a treasure trove of positive memories and a testament to the love and support that define your family's identity.

Celebrating milestones and successes is about more than marking achievements. It's about creating a culture of recognition and gratitude within your family. It's about taking the time to honor each step forward, no matter how small, and to acknowledge the strength and perseverance that have carried you through. In doing so, you uplift each other and strengthen the foundation upon which your family is built, ensuring it remains resilient and united in the face of life's challenges.

Maintaining Hope and Positivity for the Future

In the middle of life's uncertainties, it's easy to feel overwhelmed by the past and anxious about what's ahead. Yet, cultivating an optimistic mindset can be a powerful antidote to these feelings. It's about seeing the possibilities beyond the challenges, focusing on the sunlight instead of the shadows. One way to nurture this mindset is through daily affirmations—simple, positive statements reinforcing hope and resilience. As you go about your day, remind yourself of the strength you possess and the bright future that awaits. Try saying, "I can create a joyful life for myself and my children." These words, repeated often, can transform your inner dialogue and gradually shift your perspective towards positivity.

Another tool for fostering optimism is creating a vision board. Gather images and words representing your hopes and dreams, and arrange them on a board where you can see them daily. This visual reminder keeps your aspirations at the forefront of your mind, offering clarity and encouragement during tough times. A vision board is more than just a collage; it's a tangible representation of your future, a beacon of hope guiding you forward. Every time you glance at it, you're reminded of the life you're working towards, reinforcing your commitment to making it a reality.

Resilience and adaptability go hand in hand with optimism. Life is unpredictable, and challenges are inevitable, but resilience allows you to navigate these hurdles confidently. Think of resilience as a muscle that strengthens with use. By facing adversity head-on, you build the fortitude to overcome future obstacles. Drawing inspiration from stories of others who have triumphed over difficulties can be incredibly uplifting. Whether it's a biography of someone who has overcome incredible odds or a podcast sharing tales of personal triumph, these stories can remind you that you're not alone and that perseverance pays off. Engaging in resilience-building activities, like team challenges or problem-solving games, can also help develop this critical skill. These activities teach you to think on your feet, adapt to new situations, and find creative solutions, all of which contribute to a resilient mindset.

Continuous learning and growth are essential for maintaining hope and positivity. Embracing lifelong learning doesn't mean returning to school but staying curious and open to new experiences. Explore a new hobby, whether painting, cooking, or learning a musical instrument. These activities can ignite passion and provide a welcome distraction from daily stresses. Attending workshops or seminars that focus on personal growth can also be transformative. These events offer opportunities to learn new skills, meet like-minded individuals, and gain fresh perspectives on life. By committing to continuous learning, you empower yourself to grow beyond your current circumstances, expanding your horizons and increasing your capacity for joy.

Building a supportive community is another cornerstone of a positive outlook. Surround yourself with individuals who uplift and encourage you and share your values and aspirations. Joining community groups with shared interests can provide a sense of belonging and connection. Whether it's a book club, a hiking group, or a volunteer organization, these communities offer companionship and support. They remind you that you're part of something larger than yourself. Creating a network of friends and mentors can provide guidance and encouragement when needed. These relationships offer emotional support, practical advice, and insights, helping you navigate life's challenges more easily.

Visual Element: Affirmation Card Set

Consider creating a set of affirmation cards. Write a positive statement on each card, focusing on various aspects of life, such as parenting, personal growth, or resilience. Pull a card each morning to set a positive tone for your day, using it as a touchstone to keep hope alive.

Maintaining hope and positivity is about weaving a tapestry of optimism, resilience, learning, and community. It's about choosing to see the light even in the darkest moments and believing in the strength of your spirit to carry you through. By embracing these practices, you enhance your well-being and create a nurturing environment for your children, showing them the power of hope and the beauty of a life lived with intention and love.

CONCLUSION

As we end our journey together, I want to reflect on our path. When I set out to write this book, my heart was filled with a desire to help families like yours navigate the challenges of raise children after divorce. I wanted to create a resource offering practical strategies, emotional support, and understanding. Throughout these pages, we've explored the many facets of raising children in two households, from managing emotions and communication to handling legal and financial matters.

We've delved into the unique needs of children at different ages, recognizing that parenting strategies must evolve as our kids grow. We've discussed the importance of fostering resilience, adapting to new family structures, and nurturing the bonds with extended family members. We've also emphasized the critical role of self-care for parents, acknowledging that you can't pour from an empty cup.

I hope that the tools and insights shared in this book have resonated with you and that you feel empowered to implement them in your co-parenting journey.

Remember, this book is not meant to be a one-time read but a companion you can turn to whenever you need guidance or encouragement. Don't hesitate to revisit chapters that speak to your current challenges or to explore the additional resources provided.

As you move forward, I encourage you to embrace the growth and learning that comes with co-parenting. There will be moments of triumph and struggle, but keep your children's well-being at the heart of your decisions. Seek support through friends, family, or professional help when needed. Remember, you are not alone in this journey.

To the moms, dads, grandparents, and all the caregivers reading this book, I want to express my deepest gratitude. Your commitment to your children's happiness and stability is truly inspiring. By investing your time and energy into creating a nurturing co-parenting environment, you are giving your kids an incredible gift—the security of knowing they are loved and supported, no matter what.

As you close this book, I hope you do so with renewed hope and confidence. The road ahead may not always be smooth. Still, with compassion, communication, and a focus on your children's needs, you can create a family dynamic that allows everyone to thrive. Keep an open heart and mind, and trust in the power of your love for your children to guide you through any challenges that arise.

Your co-parenting journey is unique, and there is no one-size-fits-all solution. Take the strategies and ideas that resonate with you and adapt them to fit your family's needs. Don't be afraid to try new approaches or seek additional resources that align with your values and goals. The more tools you have in your co-parenting toolbox, the better equipped you'll be to handle whatever life throws your way.

Above all, remember that your children are resilient, and with your love and guidance, they can thrive in the face of change. Every small step you take towards creating a positive co-parenting dynamic is a step towards a brighter future for your family. Celebrate the milestones, learn from the setbacks, and never lose sight of the incredible difference you're making in your children's lives.

As you continue on this path, know you have a community of fellow co-parents cheering you on. Consider joining support groups, online forums, or local organizations helping families navigate divorce and co-parenting. These connections can provide invaluable encouragement, advice, and perspective when needed.

And so, my dear reader, I invite you to step forward into this new chapter of your life with courage and optimism. Embrace the possibilities and trust in your ability to create a loving, stable environment for your children. Raise Children After Divorce is not always easy, but it is worthwhile. With every hug, every heart-to-heart talk, and every milestone celebrated, you are shaping your children's lives in profound and beautiful ways.

Author: Daniel McMahon

Thank you for allowing me to be a part of your journey. I am honored to share these pages with you, and I hope the insights and strategies within will serve you well. Remember, you've got this. You are stronger than you know, and your love for your children will guide you through any darkness.

Here's to your family's happiness, resilience, and endless potential. May your co-parenting journey be filled with growth, understanding, and, above all, love.

ABOUT THE AUTHOR

I'm a single father navigating the complexities of co-parenting two foster children with his ex-wife. As a dedicated foster parent, I understand the mental and physical challenges that come with raising children who have faced their unique struggles. Balancing these responsibilities while managing the dynamics of a co-parenting relationship with an ex-wife who has mental health issues adds additional layers of difficulty but also moments of growth and resilience.

Though life after divorce is challenging, I'm committed to providing stability and love for my children. I recognize that even in difficult circumstances, co-parenting is a shared journey. With a passion for helping others, I share my experiences to provide support and insight to those facing similar struggles in fostering and post-divorce co-parenting.

I aim to be real and honest, never claiming to be perfect but always striving to create a positive, understanding environment for my children.

With gratitude and support,

Daniel McMahon

SOURCE MATERIAL

1. Afifi, T. O., Boman, J., Fleisher, W., & Sareen, J. (2009). Parental divorce or separation and children's mental health. *Journal of Psychiatric Research*, *43*(9), 768–776. https://doi.org/10.1016/j.jpsychires.2008.10.003

2. Cherry, K. (2022). 25 fun mindfulness activities for children & teens (+tips!). *PositivePsychology.com*. https://positivepsychology.com/mindfulness-for-children-kids-activities/

3. Knight, C. (2023). Erikson's stages of psychosocial development. *StatPearls*. https://www.ncbi.nlm.nih.gov/books/NBK556096/

4. Merkley, M. (2021). Positive coparenting strategies. *Utah State University Extension*. https://extension.usu.edu/relationships/faq/positive-coparenting-strategies

5. Williams, J. (2023). What are the best co-parenting apps and resources? *Futuramo*. https://futuramo.com/blog/what-are-the-best-co-parenting-apps-and-resources/

6. Kaplan, S. (2021). Co-parenting after divorce: Strategies for effective communication and conflict resolution. *KLG Florida*. https://klgflorida.com/blog/co-parenting-after-divorce-strategies-for-effective-communication-and-conflict-resolution/

7. OurFamilyWizard. (2023). Co-parenting conflict resolution techniques. *OurFamilyWizard*. https://www.ourfamilywizard.com/blog/co-parenting-conflict-resolution-techniques

8. Office of the Privacy Commissioner of Canada. (2019). 12 quick online privacy tips for parents. *Office of the Privacy Commissioner of Canada.* https://www.priv.gc.ca/en/about-the-opc/what-we-do/awareness-campaigns-and-events/privacy-education-for-kids/fs-fi/tips/

9. Custody X Change. (2023). Types of custody: Full, sole, primary, joint & more. *Custody X Change.* https://www.custodyxchange.com/topics/custody/types/custody-types.php

10. The American Bar Association. (2023). What to look for in a great family lawyer. *Law Practice Today.* https://www.americanbar.org/groups/law_practice/resources/law-technology-today/2023/what-to-look-for-in-a-great-family-lawyer/

11. Stogsdill Law Firm. (2022). Courtroom etiquette in a high-conflict divorce. *The Stogsdill Law Firm.* https://www.stogsdilllaw.com/divorce-lawyers-dupage/courtroom-etiquette-in-a-high-conflict-divorce

12. Hall Navarro. (2023). Benefits of mediation in divorce cases. *Hall Navarro.* https://hallnavarro.com/the-8-benefits-of-mediation-in-divorce-cases/

13. Shulman Law Firm. (2023). Top 5 budget apps for your post-divorce financial goals. *Shulman Law Firm.* https://shulman.ca/blog/finances/top-5-budget-apps-for-your-post-divorce-financial-goals

14. SmartAsset. (2023). How is child support calculated in New York? *SmartAsset.* https://smartasset.com/personal-finance/how-is-child-support-calculated-in-ny

15. Internal Revenue Service. (2023). Divorced and separated parents | Earned income tax credit. *Internal Revenue Service.*

https://www.eitc.irs.gov/tax-preparer-toolkit/frequently-asked-questions/divorced-and-separated-parents/divorced-and

16. Domestic Truth Foundation. (2023). 9.2 Financial planning for single or co-parenting families. *Domestic Truth Foundation.* https://domestictruthfoundation.org/courses/parenting-and-family-dynamics/lessons/9-2-financial-planning-for-single-or-co-parenting-families/

17. Zero to Three. (2022). Talking to very young children about divorce. *Zero to Three.* https://www.zerotothree.org/resource/talking-to-very-young-children-about-divorce/

18. MU Extension. (2023). Helping preteens and adolescents adjust to divorce. *Missouri University Extension.* https://extension.missouri.edu/publications/gh6616

19. Sandler, I. N. (2020). Parenting, coparenting, and adolescents' sense of autonomy. *Journal of Family Psychology, 35*(4), 567–580. https://doi.org/10.1037/fam0000590

20. Borba, M. (2023). Supporting young adults in their transition to independence. *Psychology Today.* https://www.psychologytoday.com/us/blog/promoting-empathy-with-your-teen/202401/supporting-young-adults-in-their-transition-to

21. Wolchik, S. A., Sandler, I. N., & Millsap, R. E. (2009). Promoting resilience in youth from divorced families. *Journal of Family Psychology, 23*(5), 714–720. https://doi.org/10.1037/a0016290

22. Dealing in Feelings. (2021). Creative ways to help children express emotions. *Dealing in Feelings.*

https://dealinginfeelings.com/creative-ways-to-help-children-express-emotions/

23. American Psychological Association. (2023). How to help children and teens manage their stress. *American Psychological Association.* https://www.apa.org/topics/children/stress

24. Nottage & Ward. (2023). Creating a stable environment for children post-divorce. *Nottage & Ward.* https://www.nottageandward.com/blog/allocation/creating-a-stable-environment-for-children-post-divorce/

25. Das, M. (2022). How and when to introduce your new partner to your kids. *Psychology Today.* https://www.psychologytoday.com/us/blog/a-better-divorce/202205/how-and-when-to-introduce-your-new-partner-to-your-kids

26. Acupful. (2023). Fostering positive relationships among step-siblings. *Acupful.* https://acupful.com/fostering-positive-relationships-among-step-siblings/

27. Jackson, T. (2023). When is a stepparent overstepping boundaries? *Verywell Mind.* https://www.verywellmind.com/when-is-a-stepparent-overstepping-boundaries-5216349

28. Dashnaw, D. (2022). Creating new family traditions: Building bonds in a blended family. *Daniel Dashnaw Couples Therapy.* https://danieldashnawcouplestherapy.com/blog/creating-new-family-traditions-building-bonds-in-a-blended-family

29. Minnesota Spokesman-Recorder. (2022). When a grandparent becomes co-parent. *Minnesota Spokesman-Recorder.*

https://spokesman-recorder.com/2022/11/15/when-a-grandparent-becomes-co-parent/

30. Hobson Law Firm. (2023). Coping with extended family during a break-up, separation, or divorce. *The Hobson Law Firm.* https://thehobsonlawfirm.com/coping-with-extended-family-during-a-break-up-separation-or-divorce/

31. Main Line Divorce Mediator. (2023). 8 ways to build a positive co-parenting relationship after divorce. *Main Line Divorce Mediator.* https://www.mainlinedivorcemediator.com/healthy-divorce-blog/8-ways-to-build-a-positive-co-parenting-relationship-after-divorce

32. OurFamilyWizard. (2023). OurFamilyWizard – Best co-parenting app for child custody. *OurFamilyWizard.* https://www.ourfamilywizard.com/

33. Birchwood Counseling. (2023). 5 easy self-care tips for busy parents. *Birchwood Counseling.* https://www.birchwoodcounseling.com/post/5-easy-self-care-tips-for-busy-parents

34. Seleni Institute. (2018). Managing the stress of co-parenting after divorce. *Seleni Institute.* https://seleni.org/advice-support/2018/3/20/managing-the-stress-of-co-parenting-after-divorce

35. Robbins, M. (2023). Dealing with parental guilt in divorce. *Michael A. Robbins, PLLC.* https://www.michaelarobbins.com/blog/2023/06/dealing-with-parental-guilt-in-divorce/

36. Raising Children Network. (2023). Support for parents: Why it's important and where to get it. *Raising Children Network.* https://raisingchildren.net.au/grown-

ups/services-support/about-services-support/support-for-parents-why-its-important

37. OurFamilyWizard. (2023). Creating a perfect parenting plan in 6 steps. *OurFamilyWizard*. https://www.ourfamilywizard.com/blog/creating-perfect-parenting-plan-6-steps

38. Bremer Whyte Brown & O'Meara. (2020). The importance of consistency for children after divorce. *Bremer Whyte Family Law Blog*. https://www.bremerwhytefamily.com/blog/2020/june/the-importance-of-consistency-for-children-after/

39. FamilyKind. (2023). Services for families going through divorce. *FamilyKind*. https://www.familykind.org/

40. Vogels, E. A., & Anderson, M. (2020). Parenting children in the age of screens. *Pew Research Center*. https://www.pewresearch.org/internet/2020/07/28/parenting-children-in-the-age-of-screens/

41. Burke, A. (2021). How to talk with kids about diversity and inclusion. *Whole Child Counseling*. https://www.wholechildcounseling.com/post/how-to-talk-with-kids-about-diversity-and-inclusion

42. Segal, J., & Robinson, L. (2021). Blended family and stepparenting tips. *HelpGuide*. https://www.helpguide.org/family/parenting/step-parenting-blended-families

43. Texas Education Agency. (2023). Transition next steps to independence: Skills and strategies. *Special Education Support*. https://spedsupport.tea.texas.gov/sites/default/files/2023-10/next-steps-to-independence-skills-and-strategies.pdf

44. It's Over Easy. (2023). How to turn your divorce into an opportunity for personal growth. *It's Over Easy.* https://www.itsovereasy.com/insights/how-to-turn-your-divorce-into-an-opportunity-for-personal-growth

45. Talkspace. (2022). How to co-parent successfully: 11 expert tips. *Talkspace.* https://www.talkspace.com/blog/how-to-co-parent/

46. Goldberg & Associates. (2023). Establishing a new normal for your family after divorce. *Goldberg & Associates.* https://gbfamilylaw.com/blogs/post-divorce-family-relationships-establishing-a-new-normal-for-your-family-after-divorce/

47. Utah State University Extension. (2023). How to merge traditions, celebrations and milestones in a stepfamily. *Utah State University Extension.* https://extension.usu.edu/hru/blog/how-to-merge-traditions-celebrations-and-milestones-in-a-stepfamily

www.ingramcontent.com/pod-product-compliance
Lightning Source LLC
Chambersburg PA
CBHW011550070526
44585CB00023B/2531